The Nature of Computing

Published by Crossbridge Books
Worcester
www.crossbridgeeducational.com

ISBN 978-1-913946-88-3

British Library Cataloguing Publication Data

A catalogue record for this book is available from the British Library

CROSSBRIDGE
BOOKS

The Nature of Computing

Dr. Colin B. Price

Preface

Apologia. The truth is, I didn't really want to write this text. So, how comes you are reading it now?

It's really a simple story. I rarely re-use my teaching materials from year to year, since my students always throw up new ideas and challenges many of which find their way into next-year's class. So, every new year, new students, new discussions and new research enter into my teaching space which is always dynamic.

Writing a textbook would kill this creative development. I have been there before; a long time ago I wrote a Physics textbook based on my research with students, then when it was published, I resigned. I could not teach from my own book, the same material over and over again.

So why this book? Truth is, it will soon be time for me to move on and focus on research. I must pass my classes onto new colleagues. So, this book is intended to share my mind with them, to show them one way of teaching their classes.

Fortunately, in writing this book, something strange happened; additional ideas, concepts and lessons popped into my head. So, I can still do new things next academic year, and add a few more chapters into the next edition, and so on. In Computing, we call this 'recursion'.

What is this book about and who should buy it? This book supports a 3rd-year module at the University of Worcester, UK 'Nature of Computing'. It is intended for future Worcester students, though I hope that some material may be of wider interest. You will find that I cite no academic sources; this is the job of my students as part of their assignments.

Software and Hardware used. A number of free pieces of software are mentioned in this book. We make extensive use of Octave in plotting and image processing [1], Lily pad for computational fluid dynamics [2] and Floris for investigations into wind farms [3]. In the final chapter we make use of FreeRTOS which is distributed under the MIT open-source license [4], and OpenMP [5]. In addition to our in-house robot, we use the Parallax Activity bot [6], supplemented with the Pixy2 camera [7]. We also make use of the Webots simulation framework [8].

Additional Materials. Teaching resources including worksheets and computer code are available from the author at c.price@worc.ac.uk who will send you a link to the module website. This includes files for laser-cutting a 2-wheeled stepper motor robot.

Acknowledgements. I would like to thank my past students on this module (2021-22) for their contributions to this book. Their work in class has inspired (and challenged me), and their critical eagle-eye review of my text, as it emerged, was incredibly useful. Thanks to all 52 of you; you know who you are! I would like to thank one of my other students **Flynn Osborne** who worked closely with me in various aspects of design, development and testing the materials used in this book. This included writing computer code, conducting and analysing simulations and constructing physical robots. Finally, I would like to thank my colleague **Pete Moody** for co-teaching many classes enthusiastically.

References

[1] John W. Eaton, David Bateman, Søren Hauberg, Rik Wehbring (2019). GNU Octave version 5.2.0 manual: a high-level interactive language for numerical computations.

https://www.gnu.org/software/octave/doc/v5.2.0/

[2] G D Weymouth. Lily pad: Towards real-time interactive computational fluid dynamics. In Volker Bertram & Emilio F. Campana, editor, 18th Numerical Towing Tank Symposium, Cortona Italy, 28-30 September 2015.

https://github.com/weymouth/lily-pad

[3] FLORIS. Version 2.4 (2021). Available at

https://github.com/NREL/floris.

[4] FreeRTOS available at

https://www.freertos.org/index.html

[5] Chandra, R. et al., 2001. *Parallel programming in OpenMP,* Morgan kaufmann.

[6] https://www.parallax.com/education/robotics/

[7] https://pixycam.com/pixy2/

[8] Webots, an open-source mobile robot simulation software developed by Cyberbotics Ltd.

http://www.cyberbotics.com

Contents

Page

8. Neural Circuits

9. Neural Oscillators

10. Parallel Computing

Chapter 1
Image Processing

1.1 A brief Introduction

Image processing is a huge area of application and research; important applications are in medicine, where image processing can increase the quality of an image to improve the clinician's diagnosis. Industrial applications involve object detection, looking for cracks in pipes, or sorting fruit coming down a conveyor belt according to size. Many applications are automated, or at least semi-automated, but some require human intervention to set parameters to achieve near-optimal results. You will experience all of this.

Here we shall use Octave as our toolkit; it is convenient, open source and has a huge library of functions, you will not need to write any code, but Octave is easy to read and understand. One alternative is Open-CV which integrates with Visual Studio; if you are a coder and find you enjoy image processing, then this could be a useful platform with which to develop your skills.

Images are 2D-arrays of 'pixels', where each pixel may correspond to one or more bytes; a color image, e.g., RGB will have 3 bytes per pixel, one per color channel. Octave allows us to process each channel independently, or together based on our needs. A greyscale image (no color) will have one byte per pixel, so its values will range from 0 (black) to 255 (white). Sometimes we shall work with normalized greyscale images where black is 0.0 and white is 1.0. Yep, these are floats.

We shall be covering two areas of image processing; first **image enhancement** which is all about increasing the information transfer from the image to the viewer. Here we shall be using medical images with a view of helping a radiologist make a diagnosis. The second area is **object**

detection which involves finding objects in a cluttered image, and reporting on the objects detected, such as their number and size. You will soon learn that images are corrupted by *noise* which comes from the camera sensor; we this processing.

1.2 Image Enhancement – Pixel Operations

Contrast Stretching

Consider the thorax x-ray image shown in Fig.1.1. You can clearly see there is a total lack of contrast in this image making diagnosis impossible. Just looking at the image you can see that there are many grey-ish pixels and almost no black or white pixels.

This is made clear by looking at the *histogram* of the grey-level distribution shown in Fig.1.2 for this image. Along the bottom of this plot, you find the possible grey level values for this image; it has been *normalized* so these levels range from 0.0 to 1.0. Up the side you find the number of pixels in the image with each of these possible values. So, you can see that the pixels lie in a range about $0.5 - 0.73$ which is a small part of the total range $0.0 - 1.0$. These pixels have grey-ish values.

It's easy to understand how to enhance this image. The range of pixels needs to be increased from $0.5 = 0.73$ to $0.0 - 1.0$. So, the value of each pixel has to be individually changed. How this is computed is explained using the graph below.

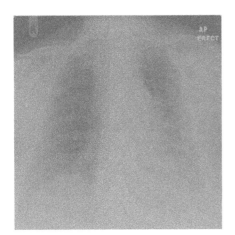

Figure 1.1 Grey-scale thorax image with lack of contrast.

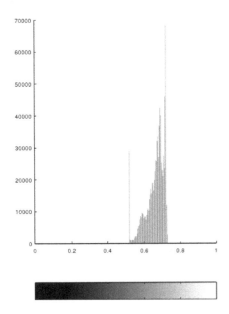

Figure 1.2 Histogram of the image in Figure 1.1

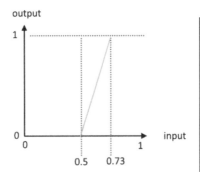

Input pixel values are mapped to output values by a linear function. Here 0.5 (in) is mapped onto 0.0 (out) and 0.73 (in) is mapped onto 1.0 (out). So the entire range of input values is stretched out

The result of this transformation is shown in Fig.1.3 with the associated histogram in Fig.1.4. Looking at the image, you can see a dramatic improvement in its appearance; if images could speak (and they can when you look at them), this one has much more to say. You can see the ribs, collar bones and other features including the heart. Also, there is a small cancer nodule, that white circle, in the lung region on the left.

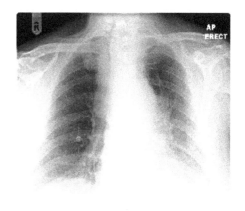

Figure 1.3 Contrast Stretched Image

The histogram shows that the stretching operation has changed the distribution of grey values which are now spread over the entire available range, 0.0 – 1.0. So the image is being used more optimally to convey information to the viewer. All is not perfect; some pixels are not present in the image as shown by the gaps in the histogram.

Perhaps you could think of a way to improve this, using some sort of interpolation to fill in the missing pixels?

Automatic Contrast Stretching

It is always interesting to see if when a human has made a decision on parameter values, whether this could be automated by some computer algorithm. For contrast stretching this is straightforward. A program could look at all the grey values in an image and find the lowest and the highest. It would then map these values onto the full range of 0.0 – 1.0. Octave has a function

```
stretchlim(image);
```

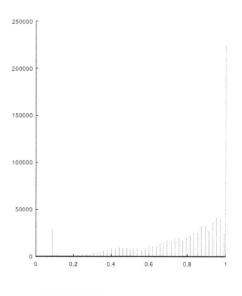

which returns the lowest value (+1%) and the highest value (-1%). This range can then be used by a second function

```
imadjust(I,[lowIn,highIn],[lowOut,highOut]);
```

to do the actual mapping. This automation clearly corresponds to the discussion above.

Figure 1.4 Histogram of Contrast Stretched Image

Histogram Equalization

We have seen how contrast stretching *implicitly* changes the histogram of grey values. This raises the question – can we *explicitly* change the histogram to improve the image. The answer is yes, and this is 'histogram equalization'. The basic idea is that an image communicates *information* to the viewer, and that pixel grey values do this communication. So how can we make this optimal? Well, the first thing is to make sure we use the entire range of grey values, as discussed above. The second thing is to try to change the grey values so the number of pixels with each grey value is about the same. This ensures that each grey value is being used equally as often, and so the maximum amount of information is being communicated. Here's an example applied to the 'Lena' image (Fig.1.5).

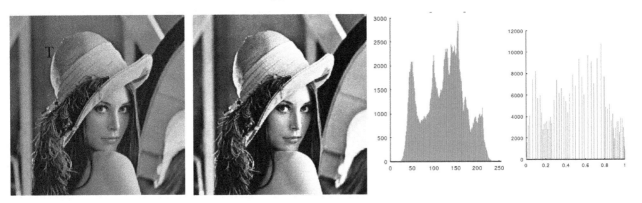

Figure 1.5 Histogram Equalization: Left image before and after, right histogram before and after

The results are not as spectacular as one would hope; while contrast stretching has been obtained, the numbers of pixels with each grey value is certainly not the same. Comparing the two histograms you may see that the peaks and troughs have been smoothed out, and that the histogram has been *partially* equalized.

Histogram equalization is popular in many areas of image processing, especially industrial applications. One area where it is not widely used is in medical applications since it is a very 'brutal' transformation, often producing large areas of very bright or very dark pixels. You can see this in Fig.1.6 where we have applied histogram equalization to the thorax image from Fig.1.1.

1.3 Image Enhancement – Spatial Filtering

The image processing operations we have seen so far have worked on *individual pixels*. Now we turn to a class of operations which process *regions* of pixels. Let's see how the approach works using a diagrammatic representation of an image. The computation works like this; the **kernel** is scanned across all pixels in the image from top-left to bottom right, and at each pixel there is a computation. For the example shown in Fig.1.7, the *inputs* to the computation are the 9 image pixels lying underneath the kernel cells, and the *output* from the computation is located at the centre kernel cell in the output image.

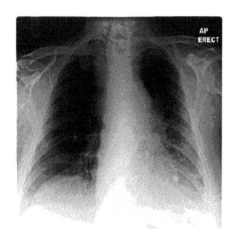

Figure 1.6 Histogram equalization applied to the thorax image in Fig.1.1.

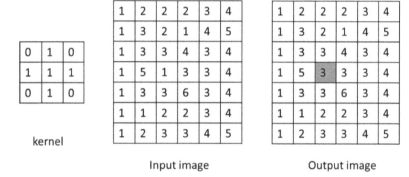

Figure 1.7 Convolution with a 3x3 kernel. The pixel shaded red is the output pixel.

Here the kernel has scanned over part of the image and is sitting on top of the yellow shaded area. The computation is simple; each kernel number is multiplied by the underlying pixel value, and the results are summed. Then we divide by the sum of the kernel values. So, we have

(0x3)+(1x3)+(0x4)+(1x5)+(1x1)+(1x3)+(0x3)+(1x3)+(0x6)

which sums to 15, and we divide by the kernel sum (5) to give us 15/5 = 3 which is the output pixel, shown in red in the output image. This process is called *convolution*.

Image Noise

Spatial filtering is mainly used to remove noise in an image. It turns out that noise is the major headache in successful image processing; removal of noise is often the first stage in an image processing pipeline of operations. Where does noise come from? First there is 'salt and pepper' noise which comes from 'dead' pixels in the imaging device, these pixels are permanently black or white due to defects in the camera sensor. Second there is Gaussian noise, a random variation of pixel values around an expected value, this noise follows a normal distribution. Both types of noise will be explored below and are illustrated in Fig.1.8.

Filtering with the 'Mean' Filter

This is very much like the example above, except that all the kernel values are set to 1.0, and we divide by the sum of these values. In general, the kernel can have size NxN (where N is always odd, so that there is a central 'output' pixel) and the kernel values are all set to

$$\frac{1}{N^2}$$

so the sum of the kernel values is 1.0. E.g., for a kernel size 3x3, its values are set to 1/9.

Applying this filter to the images in Fig.1.8 gives the results shown in Fig.1.9 where there is a clear improvement in the image quality, though the salt-and-pepper noise is still visible on the surface of the Moon. There is another filter, the 'median' filter that does a better job at removing salt-and-pepper noise, we'll see that shortly. Also, if you look carefully, you will just be able to see some blurring (smoothing) at the edge of the disk. Here is the kernel used in this example

Figure 1.8 Top, original image, centre with salt and pepper noise, bottom with Gaussian noise.

```
0.11111   0.11111   0.11111
0.11111   0.11111   0.11111
0.11111   0.11111   0.11111
```

To understand the effects of the mean filter, we shall apply it to a 1D synthetic image containing a single edge corrupted by Gaussian noise. We shall then smooth the image with kernels of increasing size. Here's the original image together with a smoothed image of kernel size 3.

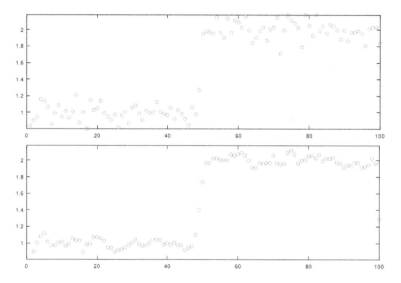

Top, noisy image, bottom results of smoothing with kernel size 3

The original image, before noise was added comprised the left half with a value of 1.0 and the right half 2.0. The effects of noise are clearly seen. After the smoothing, the size of the noise spikes has clearly been lowered, and both left and right halves are smoother. Now let's see the effects of increasing the kernel size to 7.

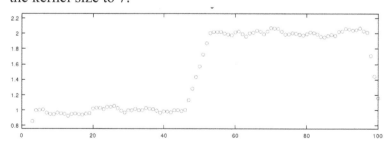

Smoothing the noisy image with kernel size 7

Figure 1.9. Images from Figure 1.8 smoothed with a mean filter with kernel size 3x3

There is much better smoothing here, but something else has changed, the central edge in the image has become less steep in other words, blurred. It's easy to understand that as the kernel size gets larger, there is better smoothing out of noise, but edges become smoothed too, which is not really desirable. There is a trade-off here.

The Gaussian Kernel

The mean filter sums image pixels under the kernel footprint with equal weight, which means that the information in the central pixel being processed is diluted with information from pixels further away. The Gaussian kernel does better being processed.

The Gaussian kernel is derived from the continuous function

$$f(x,y) = \frac{1}{2\pi\sigma^2} e^{\frac{-(x^2+y^2)}{2\sigma^2}}$$

where the centre of the kernel is at $x=0$, $y=0$. The parameter σ ('sigma') controls how quickly the kernel 'falls off' in space. Here's a couple of examples, both for kernel sizes 5x5.

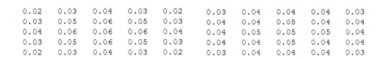

0.02	0.03	0.04	0.03	0.02		0.03	0.04	0.04	0.04	0.03
0.03	0.05	0.06	0.05	0.03		0.04	0.04	0.05	0.04	0.04
0.04	0.06	0.06	0.06	0.04		0.04	0.05	0.05	0.05	0.04
0.03	0.05	0.06	0.05	0.03		0.04	0.04	0.05	0.04	0.04
0.02	0.03	0.04	0.03	0.02		0.03	0.04	0.04	0.04	0.03

Left Gaussian kernel sigma = 2, right sigma = 3.

There are several things to note. First the kernels are *symmetric*, they have the same values in equivalent horizontal and vertical locations. Second, the values are larger near the centre, the kernels actually have a bell-like shape. Finally, you can see that for a small σ the values drop of quickly as you move out from the centre, the opposite for a larger σ.

The Median Filter

The median of a set of numbers is the midpoint of the set when it is sorted from lowest to highest number. This filter also operates on a NxN neighbourhood, and the sorting operation has to be carried out at each pixel. It turns out that this filter is superior to mean or Gaussian smoothing since it

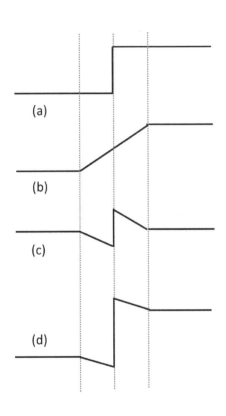

Figure 1.10 Unsharp Masking: (a) original image (b) smoothed image (c) edge image (d) final image

tends to better preserve edges, and also removes isolated noise spikes such as salt-and-pepper noise. However, it is much more computationally expensive than the averaging filters since pixel values in the kernel must be sorted for each centre (output) pixel. Compare this with the averaging filters which involve NxN multiplications and (NxN -1) additions.

1.4 Unsharp Masking

This beautiful technique finds its origins in dark-room photography and was used long before digital image processing. Its aim is to enhance the image by accentuating any edges in the image, producing a more 'crisp' image. It works by smoothing the image with a mean or Gaussian kernel, then subtracting that from the original image to extract edges in the image. This 'edge' image is then added to the original image, with some weighting, to produce the final sharpened image.

This is illustrated with a toy edge (Fig.1.10): (a) shows the original step edge, (b) after smoothing the extent of which is determined by the kernel size, (c) shows (a)-(b) which has extracted the edge, and (d) is a fraction of (c) added to (a), you can see the edge is accentuated.

Fig.1.11 shows this applied to 'Lena'. We can also write down these stages mathematically

$$I_{edge} = I_{orig} - I_{smoothed}$$

$$I_{final} = I_{orig} + \alpha I_{edge}$$

where α is typically between 0.0 and 1.0 and after a bit of maths we can simplify this

$$I_{final} = (1 + \alpha)I_{orig} - \alpha I_{smoothed}$$

This requires a smoothing kernel, followed by a subtraction of two image pixels. This can be combined into a single kernel.

Original Image

Smoothed Image

Difference Image

Orig + alpha*Difference

Figure 1.11 Unsharp Masking. Images are labelled.

1.5 Edge Detection

Detecting edges in images is a useful image processing operation and has two main applications; (i) enhancing the image as we have seen, (ii) *segmenting* the image into the objects it contains. We shall see the latter a little later on, for the moment we need to understand how to detect edges. The operation is shown in Fig.1.12 applied to some coins. The output image grey values are large (white) where there are edges. The algorithm works reasonably well, but it has also detected the edges within the coins. Again, image processing is tricky.

It is understood that the human visual system (HVS) contains a bank of edge detectors tuned to edges and lines of various widths and orientations. The outputs of these are used for object recognition.

Let's design a convolution kernel which detects edges, and let's work in 1D. In regions where the grey level is constant, e.g., a load of 1's (no edge) then the detector should output zero. In other words, the kernel should take the *difference* between nearby pixels. Here's a good candidate

This will subtract the left pixel value from the right pixel value and output the result at the centre pixel. Let's see this working on a toy image

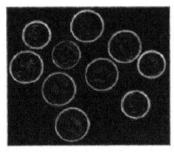

Figure 1.12 Edge detection applied to coins

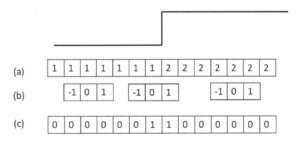

At the top is a pure edge, the left and right pixel values are shown. In the middle three positions of the kernel are shown

the first outputs 0, the second 1 and the third 0. So ,where there is no edge, the output is 0, the edge outputs a 1 on both sides of the edge. So, if we look at the output image, it would be black with the edge showing as white, rather like in Fig.1.12.

For 2D images we need a difference operator in both directions. One old workhorse is the Sobel operator, which is a pair of 3x3 kernels,

-1	0	1
-2	0	2
-1	0	1

-1	-2	-1
0	0	0
1	2	1

The left kernel finds the edges in the horizontal direction (columns) and the right kernel finds the edges in the vertical direction (rows). The Octave function `imgradient(image)` calculates both and combines the results to give the magnitude of the edge value at each pixel in the image. That's what you see in Fig.1.12.

Edge detection operators are *gradient* operators and respond to changes in image grey level height. Think of roads of various gradients, such operators (in physical space) would tell you the gradient of the road. Unfortunately, gradient operators respond rather well to noise, as you can see in the toy problem below which shows a single salt-and-pepper spike on a flat background and the result of our simple edge detector.

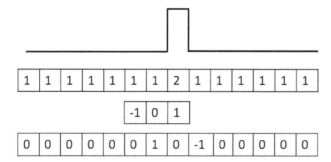

We've been here before and so we understand the problem. Before we apply the edge detector kernel, we must first smooth the image to reduce the noise, ideally using a median filter. Of course, too much smoothing will also blur the edges, and may cause some edges to run into each other.

1.6 Segmentation

Segmentation is the process of extracting objects or features from an image. Inspection of electronic circuit boards may need to check that all components are present, thus the components (chips, resistors, etc) need to be identified in the image. A simple example is shown in Fig.1.13 where the original image comprises a number of coins, the objects to be detected in an image. The goal here is to identify all coins in the image, give them a label, and calculate their areas. The image has been successfully segmented into a background layer (cyan) and each extracted coin has been labelled with a color. You can see that one coin has not been segmented exactly.

Segmentation is one of the trickiest areas in image processing and is still the subject of research, its success often depends on the quality of the input image. For industrial situations this is relatively straightforward where the engineer has some control over environmental variables (such as lighting). For remote (satellite) sensing, e.g., of land usage, this is often difficult, since the image quality is dictated by the sensing device and procedure. There are two broad approaches to segmentation (i) using edges (ii) using regions. We shall look at the latter here.

Interactive Thresholding

Think about a grey level image, Fig.1.13; this comprises pixels with values in the range 0-255. Now think of a segmented image which we can write as

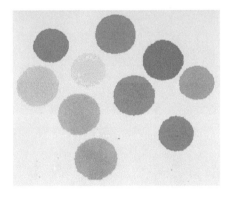

Figure 1.13 Segmentation: Top original coin image, bottom segmented and labelled coins

segmented image = objects AND background

So, a segmented image is a *binary* image where the background is 0 (black) and the objects are 1 or 255 (white).

How can we create such a binary image? We can draw on our understanding of histograms of grey values. Look at the histogram of the image in Fig.1.14. What does this tell us? Well we have two peaks, showing there are a load of darker pixels and a load of lighter pixels. Clearly the dark pixels form the background, and the lighter pixels are the objects we are segmenting out. All we need to do is to choose a *threshold* grey value to separate pixels in these peaks out. All pixels whose grey value is less than the threshold are assigned to binary 0 in the output image, those greater are assigned to 1 in the output image. Results for a threshold of 120 are shown in Fig.1.14. The result is close but not perfect. Interactive thresholding allows the user to tune the thresholding for a particular situation (image type, lighting, etc) so successive images may be correctly segmenting. But of course, we would like to automate this process.

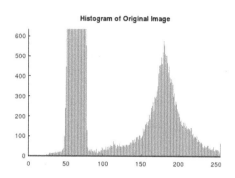

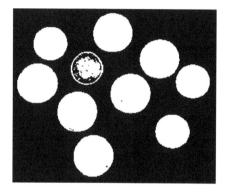

Figure 1.14 Histogram of image from Fig 1.13 with results of thresholding at 120

Automatic Processing

Here we outline an algorithm which could find the threshold automatically, and so adjust to the input image.

1. Estimate a good threshold T
2. Segment into two regions A and B
3. Compute the means of each region m_1 and m_2
4. Compute a new threshold
$$T = \frac{1}{2}(m_1 + m_2)$$
5. Repeat steps 2 to 4 until the change in the threshold is less than a specified value

Otsu's Algorithm

This method of computing the optimal threshold partitions the image pixels into two sets. Say there are L total grey values in the image. Then pixels are put into one set with values [0,1,2,…,k] and the other set with the remaining larger values [k+1, k+2, …, L-1]. Otsu then calculates a *variance*. Let's refresh ourselves what variance means. If you open a can of peas, they all have about the same mean size, differences in size from the mean is small; so we have a low variance. But look at the heights of folk in the lab; there is a well-defined mean (no-one is 3m tall) but there is quite a bit of spread in height, so quite some variance.

Now Otsu looked at the variance of the grey values of the pixels in the two initial sets, but more importantly, he looked at the variance *between* the two sets, and he argued that the best segmentation would *maximize this variance*.

Segmenting Noisy Images

We have added some serious Gaussian noise to the original coin image which now appears in Fig.1.15 where the additional noise pixels have created an image whose histogram does not have a valley; it is *unimodal* rather than the *bimodal* histogram we want. Clearly it is impossible to assign a threshold to this image. So how do we proceed? Drawing on our understanding of smoothing noisy images, let's apply a 5x5 average smoothing kernel. The smoothed image and its histogram, and the results of Otsu's algorithm are shown in Fig.1.16.

The final segmentation result is almost perfect, and Otsu's algorithm has performed exceedingly well since the histogram is quite complicated having at least two troughs. The effect of smoothing has produced a relatively larger number of brighter pixels (the coins) even though there is still a huge number of pixels in the range 160-200.

Labelling and Analysing Objects

This is quite straightforward and is explained in the diagram below. We start at the top left pixel in the image and scan across the columns, and down the rows. If we find an object pixel (value = 1) then we increment our label, and label that pixel; this is shown as yellow in the diagram. Then we continue scanning, and if we find an object pixel

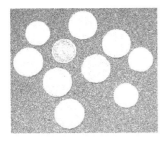

Figure 1.15 A noisy image and its histogram, Impossible to segment

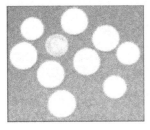

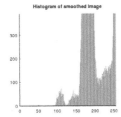

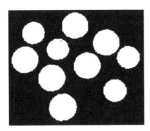

Figure 1.16 Segmentation by pre-processing smoothing followed by Otsu's algorithm

neighbouring the one, we have labelled, then we label that second pixel with the same label. You can see this in the first diagram where one pixel is labelled yellow, and the next one to the right will also be labelled yellow.

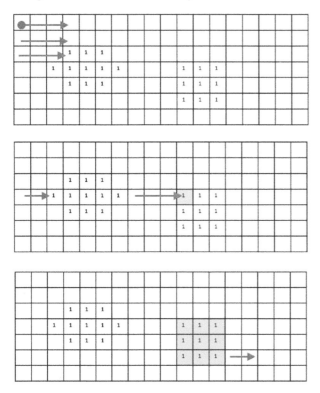

In the second diagram, the next row of the first object is complete, then we hit another object pixel. This is not connected to the first labelled object, so we assign a new label, in this case green. Finally, all objects are labelled. Once they are labelled, we can return to this list of labelled objects and do some analysis, e.g., we can count the pixels to get their area, or find the object width and height or shape.

Chapter 2
Robot Kinematics

2.1 A brief Introduction

Kinematics is the study of movement (well almost) so in this chapter we are looking at the principles of robot movement, for our 2-wheeled differential drive robot. The explanation is mathematical; this is necessary for us to write code to get the robot moving. The most important expressions are highlighted. So how does a wheeled robot move? Simply by driving its wheels. If you drive both wheels at the same angular speed, then the robot moves forward. If you drive the left wheel faster, then the robot will arc to the right. Driving both wheels at the same speed, but in opposite directions, will make the robot spin about its axis.

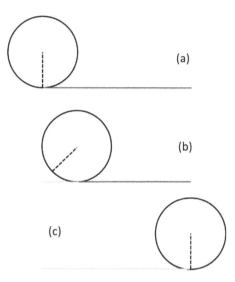

Figure 2.1. Rotating wheel leaving a track of blue paint on the surface

2.2 Linear and Angular Velocities

Let's see how wheels work. Fig.2.1 shows a wheel completing a full revolution. Imagine the type is coated with paint, so as the wheel rotates it paints a nice line on the surface. How long is this line? Simply the circumference of the wheel.

Now let's do a quick calculation. I guess you will remember the expression for the circumference of a circle radius r. This is of course $2\pi r$. So, if we have a wheel of radius 33mm then one rotation will shift the robot a distance $(2)(3.1415)(33) = 207$mm.

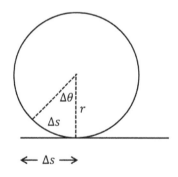

Figure 2.2. Wheel rotating with a change in angle

And now for some maths. If one rotation gives a distance of $2\pi r$ then half a rotation will give half of this distance, but what about if the angle of rotation is $\Delta\theta$? (Here the symbol Δ means a change and θ is the angle. Well, the arc of the circle corresponding to the angle $\Delta\theta$ is just

$$\Delta s = r\Delta\theta \qquad (1)$$

where the angle is in radians (more on that later). So, this is the length of the line painted by the robot, and is the distance moved forward, look at Fig.2.2.

Now let's think about the robot's speed in mm/sec. Speed is the distance moved Δs in a time interval Δt. Here's the expression for speed.

$$v = \frac{\Delta s}{\Delta t} \qquad (2)$$

Continuing with our example, if the robot wheels make one revolution in 2 seconds, then the robot speed is

$$v = \frac{2\pi r}{2} = \frac{207}{2} = 103.5 \; mm/sec$$

Try to imagine what that means. The symbol for speed is v since what we are really talking about is *velocity*, speed in a particular direction (forward or backward).

But robots move by turning their wheel with their servomotors and our computer programs must provide *drive* to the motors to make them rotate. To make a servomotor rotate, we must give it a series of 'pulses' where the pulse width determines the rotational speed. For the robot we shall be using, the 'Parallax Activity Bot /BoE Bot' the relationship between pulse width and speed is shown in the diagram below. The points show real measurements, and the

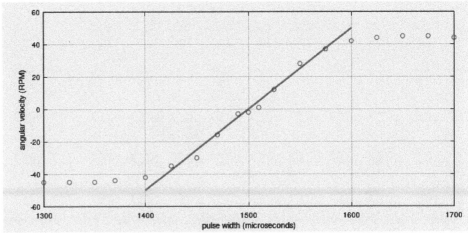

red line has been placed to capture the most useful part of the experimental curve, where speed is proportional to pulse width. You can see that with a pulse width of 1500 μs (microseconds) the motor does not rotate. Therefore, in our code (and in our thinking) we shall define a quantity **drive** *relative to this 1500*. So, a drive of 50 will create a rotational velocity of around 30 rpm, and a drive of -50 will rotate the motor at this rpm, but in the opposite direction.

It's easy to get a relationship between drive and rpm from the red line above; here we find this is

$$drive = \frac{50.0}{30.0}rpm \qquad (3)$$

In our code, you will see the variables **driveL** and **driveR** which are, of course, the drives sent to the left and right servomotors.

Now we need to understand how the values of driveL and driveR will determine the robot's speed; let's assume these are the same, so the robot will move forwards (we'll look at other possibilities later). If we stick expression (1) for the distance gone when the wheel rotates through an angle, into expression (2) which is the definition for linear robot velocity moving forward, we get

$$v = \frac{\Delta s}{\Delta t} = \frac{r\Delta\theta}{\Delta t} = r\frac{\Delta\theta}{\Delta t}$$

Here $\Delta\theta/\Delta t$ tells us how fast the wheel angle changes with time, so this is the *angular velocity* of the wheel; we give this the symbol ω so we have a fundamental expression

$$v = \omega r \qquad (4)$$

This makes sense; if the wheel radius r is increased, then the linear speed v is increased, and if the angular velocity ω is increased (the wheel rotates faster) then the linear speed is increased. All seems good, and it is. There may be a conceptual stumbling block, however, it's due to the *units* of angular velocity ω. The angle change in (1) is measured in *radians* (in one revolution, there are 360 degrees which is 2π radians, a little over 6). So, we need to connect angular velocity in radians/sec to angular velocity in rpm, so we can use the above drive graph.

Help! What are radians?

Think of a wheel rotating once, through 360 degrees. We know the distance gone is the circumference of the wheel $2\pi r$. Now expression (1) tells us that this distance is $r\Delta\theta$. So, we have

$$2\pi r = r\Delta\theta$$

and cancelling the r gives us

$$\Delta\theta = 2\pi$$

therefore, in a circle, there are 2π radians.

Let's say the wheels are rotating at n rpm, i.e., n_{rpm}. Therefore, the revs per second is

$$n_{rps} = \frac{n_{rpm}}{60}$$

Each rotation the wheel rotates 2π radians, therefore the radians per second (ω) is just

$$\omega = 2\pi \frac{n_{rpm}}{60} = \frac{2\pi}{60} n_{rpm}$$

i.e.,

$$\omega = \frac{2\pi}{60} n_{rpm} \qquad (5)$$

Let's work through an example how we would use this maths to make a robot move forwards a desired distance, in a desired time.

Let's take the case of driving the robot a desired distance of 80mm in a desired time of 2 seconds, a speed of 40 mm/s.

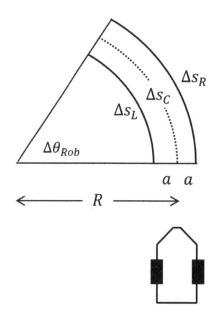

$v = \frac{\Delta s}{\Delta t}$ (2)		$v = 80/2 = 40$ mm/sec
$\omega = \frac{v}{r}$ from (4)		$\omega = 40/33.0 = 1.21$ rad/sec
$n_{rpm} = \frac{60}{2\pi}\omega$ from (5)		$n_{rpm} = (60*1.21)/6.28 = 12$ rpm
		drive $= (50.0/30.0)*12 = 20$

We shall revisit this below when we discuss how to code our robot.

2.3 Movement on an arc

Have a look at Fig.2.3, at the bottom you will see the robot. The length of its axle, connecting its wheels is $2a$ and for the Parallax robot we are using, this is 104.0 mm, so we have $a = 52$ mm.

The diagram shows that the centre of the robot (between the wheels) moves along an arc of radius R. So the left wheel moves along an arc of radius $(R - a)$ and the right wheel moves along a larger arc of radius $(R + a)$. Clearly the right wheel is moving faster than the left. The robot's *pose* changes, it started off moving North, and it ends up moving Northwest, having changed its bearing by an angle θ_{Rob}. The subscript *Rob* reminds us we are thinking about the entire robot, rather than its wheels.

To understand the maths which follows, we apply the relationship
$\Delta s = r\Delta\theta$ used above. So, for the left wheel we have

$$\Delta s_L = (R - a)\Delta\theta_{Rob} \qquad (6a)$$

and for the right wheel

Figure 2.3. Robot moving on an arc. Distance a is between each wheel and the robot centre.

$$\Delta s_R = (R + a)\Delta\theta_{Rob} \qquad (6b)$$

Now let's imagine that the robot takes a certain time interval Δt to complete its trajectory along the arc. To find the robot wheel speeds, we must divide distance gone by each wheel by this time interval, see expression (2). So, we get for the left wheel

$$v_L = \frac{\Delta s_L}{\Delta t} = (R - a)\frac{\Delta\theta_{Rob}}{\Delta t} \qquad (7a)$$

and for the right wheel

$$v_R = \frac{\Delta s_R}{\Delta t} = (R + a)\frac{\Delta\theta_{Rob}}{\Delta t} \qquad (7b)$$

This is fine, but these expressions are not really telling us much. So, we must go forwards a bit. Remember the expression (1) connecting wheel distance and angle. For the left and right wheels these become, since both wheels have the same radius.

$$\Delta s_L = r\Delta\theta_L, \quad and \quad \Delta s_R = r\Delta\theta_R$$

and putting these into expressions (7a) and (7b) we find

$$r\left(\frac{\Delta\theta_L}{\Delta t}\right) = (R - a)\left(\frac{\Delta\theta_{Rob}}{\Delta t}\right) \qquad (8a)$$

and

$$r\left(\frac{\Delta\theta_R}{\Delta t}\right) = (R + a)\left(\frac{\Delta\theta_{Rob}}{\Delta t}\right) \qquad (8b)$$

I've stuck in some brackets here, where changes in angles are divided by a corresponding change in time. These are angular velocities, speeds of rotation.

The symbol for angular velocity is **omega** ω (lower case) or Ω (upper case). Lower case ω is the angular velocity of the *wheels* and upper case Ω is the angular velocity of the robot body, when viewed from above; this is just the rotation speed of the robot.

So, we can rewrite equations (8) like this

$$r\omega_L = (R - a)\Omega_{Rob}$$

$$r\omega_R = (R + a)\Omega_{Rob}$$

therefore

$$\omega_L = \frac{(R - a)\Omega_{Rob}}{r} \qquad (9a)$$

$$\omega_R = \frac{(R + a)\Omega_{Rob}}{r} \qquad (9b)$$

These are very useful expressions. As with all expressions, think of the stuff on the right of the = sign as an *input* to a computation, what we want to calculate, and the stuff on the left is what we have to code to make this happen. So, if we want the robot to go around an arc of radius R with an angular velocity Ω_{Rob} then we have to make the motors rotate with angular velocities ω_L and ω_R.

2.4 Special Cases

There are two special cases of the maths in expressions (9). First, when the robot is moving straight, then we can write $R \to \infty$ so we can neglect a in the expressions, and R divides out. You can see this by calculating the ratio of the wheel omega's

$$\frac{\omega_L}{\omega_R} = \frac{(R - a)}{(R + a)} \qquad (10)$$

where the ratio becomes $R/R = 1$ which tells us that the omegas are the same, i.e., both wheels rotate at the same speed.

The other special case is when $R = 0$, this is where the robot rotates about its centre. Putting this into expressions (10) we find

$$\frac{\omega_L}{\omega_R} = -1 \qquad (11)$$

so, the omegas are equal and opposite!

A Worked Example

Let's say we want our robot to travel along an arc of radius 300mm and change its pose by 45 degrees, and it does this in 2 seconds, see Fig. 2.4.

The angle expressed in radians is $45\pi/180 = 0.785$rad. The angular velocity of the robot Ω_{Rob} is $0.785/2.0 = 0.393$ rad/sec.

Since $a = 52$mm for the Parallax robot and our arc has a radius of 300 mm, plugging these into expressions (8) gives us

$$\omega_L = \frac{(300 - 52)0.393}{33}, \quad \omega_R = \frac{(300 + 52)0.393}{33}$$

and so, we calculate

$$\omega_L = 2.85 \ rad/s, \quad \omega_R = 4.19 \ rad/s$$

Now we need to convert these *omegas* to *rpms*. Since an omega of 2π rad/s corresponds to 1 rev/sec, then 1 rad/s corresponds to $1/2\pi$ rev/sec. Then ω rad/s corresponds to $\omega/2\pi$ rev/sec, and therefore to $60\omega/2\pi$ rpm. To get revs per second we divide the omegas by 2π which gives us

left 0.45 revs/sec   right 0.67 revs/sec

and to get the revs/min we multiply by 60

left 27 revs/min   right   40.2 revs/min

and using the expression (3) for drive, we finally have

left drive 45   right drive 67

which are the drive signals we send to our motors.

All of these calculations are done in our Arduino code. The purpose of this worked example is simply to explain what the code actually does.

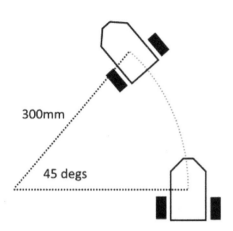

Figure 2.4 Worked example. The robot rotates 45 degs on an arc 300mm and takes 2 seconds.

2.5 How to Code a Real Robot

We need to get the robot to move forward a certain distance we specify or rotate an angle we specify or rotate on an arc. In our code, we have to specify **drives** which will make the robot move as we want, then send these drives to the servos. Here's a code snippet which gets the robot moving forwards

```
driveL = 30;
driveR = 30;
driveServos(driveL,driveR);
```

This code will get the robot moving (for ever) but we would rather like to tell the robot *how far to move* and *with what speed*. So, here's some code to get the robot moving forward for a specified distance (in mm) over a specified time. We relate the code to the corresponding maths. All the variables have been declared for you in the code templates.

`desDist = 80;`	
`desTime = 2.0;`	
`desSpeed = desDist/desTime;`	expression (2)
`omega = desSpeed/wheelRad;`	from expression (4)
`rpm = (60/(2*PI))*omega;`	from expression (5)
`driveL = (50.0/30.0)*rpm;`	expression (3)
`driveR = driveL;`	
`driveServos(driveL,driveR);`	
`delayTime = (int)(desTime*1000)`	
`delay(delayTime);`	
`driveServos(0.0,0.0);`	

The last three lines deserve some comment. The lines before them set the motor drives and therefore their speeds. These last three lines specify how long the servos must spin. So we calculate the **delayTime** in milliseconds from our **desTime** (in seconds), and pass it to the **delay(...)** function which suspends the MPU for this time. Then, we drive the servos with driveL = 0.0 and driveR = 0.0 which will make them stop. So, the final result is that the robot will move 80mm forwards and it will take 2secs to do this, both values we specify.

Now the maths is perfect, and the code is perfect (they are both perfect *abstract* systems of thinking), but when you get the robot to execute this code, it will not move 80mm forwards, it will be more, or it will be less. Why? Because the robot is not *abstract*, it is not a *simulation*, it is really *embodied in the real world*. Think of its motors, their datasheet may specify their 'accuracy' as 10%. This means that if you ask them to rotate with an angular velocity of 10 rpm, they will rotate with anywhere between 9 and 11 rpm. In the worst-case scenario, the left motor could rotate at 9 rpm and the right at 11 rpm; the robot would not go straight forward but arc to the left! Also, we need to know the wheel radius, and so we measure it, but our measurements are subject to errors. Also the relationship between **drive** and rpm may not be the one we presented earlier, each motor is different. Looking at the drive-rpm curve again (reproduced below) we see a real issue.

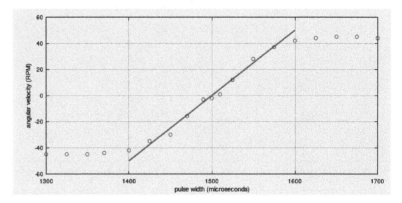

If we look at pulse Width 1500 (drive = 0) we see that increasing the drive to about 20 does not make the motor turn! There is a 'dead band'. This means that we cannot use small forward drives or motor speeds.

So, back to our problem. There are two ways to cope with this problem: The first relies on direct observation of the robot, and measurement of how it moves. Let's say we ask the robot to move 80mm and we measure how far it moves, 90mm; it's gone too far. So we could reduce the wheel velocity **omega**, but we know this is dangerous, since if omega is made too small, then the motor will not turn.

There is another way to make the robot travel less far; we can reduce the amount of time we drive the motors. So, we change the **desTime**

```
correctionFactor = desDist/actualDist;
desTime = desTime*correctionFactor;
```

It is important that we make this change at the appropriate place in the code, it must not be made before we calculate the omega's since they depend on the desTime. Here's where to put the correction, so that it only affects the **delayTime** which tells the motors how long to rotate.

```
correctionFactor = desDist/actualDist;


desTime = desTime*correctionFactor;
delayTime = (int)(desTime*1000)
delay(delayTime);
driveServos(0.0,0.0);
```

Chapter 3
Robot Vision

3.1 A brief Introduction

Mobile robot perception is an interesting field of study and has evolved from ad-hoc solutions to specific robot situations to more grounded theory. Robots can be equipped with human-like senses (vision, sound, touch) but these can be supplemented with various others. Ultrasonic 'ping' rangefinders are perhaps inspired by the bat, motion detection by the fly eye. The compass could be likened to bird-brain sensory areas; it's interesting to look for natural analogues of other sensors such as GPS, wheel encoders, gyroscopes, laser rangefinders and doppler sensors.

Sensors can be classified as **exteroceptive**, those which respond to the external environment, such as vision, and **proprioceptive**, those which respond the robot's insides, such as battery voltage, wheel position and wheel load. Human vision is both a powerful sensory medium and is incredibly difficult to mimic in a robotics context; remember that over 50% of our brain is devoted to solving vision problems. Compared with other sensors, such as laser range-finding which responds to one (or a few) objects in a scene, robot vision has the potential to give information about the entire scene structure. The laser range-finder sends out a *ray,* and its collision with an object occurs at a particular angle and distance, whereas a camera has a *field of view* and can report all objects within that field. Usually images are processed before analysis; this may include edge-detection, segmentation and object labelling, or specific transforms which return information about straight lines, extracted by combing edges (Hough transform).

3.2 Limitations

First, we must accept the limitations of developing Computer Vision solutions for the small mobile robots, often based on Arduino technology we encounter. The first limitation is memory size. Consider a small image of resolution 300x200 with three colour channels, i.e., 3 bytes per pixel, which requires 180 kB of storage. The Arduino Mega2560 has 8 kB of data memory; clearly you cannot run image processing algorithms on this MPU, since there cannot be an image in memory! The second limitation is processing speed; take a 300x200 grey-scale image, performing a convolution with a 3x3 kernel, at a rate of 60 fps, requires a MPU clock speed of over 60 MHz whereas the Arduino gives us 16 MHz.

How can this be solved? Some companies offer Arduino-compatible alternatives with huge memory and fast processors (e.g, the Maixduino has 8 MB of data memory and runs at 400 MHz and retails at around £25). These boards mainly use the STMicroelectronics 'Cortex' MCU which is industry standard; the Maixduino board supplements this with a Kendryte AI processor. Compared with the Arduino, these boards are often tricky to bring into service, and documentation and blogs are hard to find, however we have had recent success getting the Maixduino up and running using PlatformIO. Then, of course, we could cross over to the dark-side and use a Raspberry-Pi, or even the NVIDIA Jetson technology.

Another solution is to off-load vision processing to a dedicated board, which applies one or more image processing algorithms, and sends the extracted features (such as segmented object sizes) to the Arduino for analysis. A feature can be coded in a few bytes, so memory space and transfer and processing rates is not an issue. This is the solution we shall encounter, our 'Pixy2' camera and processing board, which runs algorithms to (i) detect coloured blobs and return their location and size, (ii) detect lines, returning their endpoints as (x,y) coordinates in the image, (iii) detect types of intersections between lines. These are useful functions for a Robot Vision system, as we shall see. In addition, Pixy2 lets us extract individual pixels from the image, so we could just about code our own algorithm, e.g., a multi-line detector. This device is impressive, it boasts a dual-core 204 MHz NXP LPC4330 processor with an Aptina MT9M114 1296 x 976 resolution camera.

3.3 Pin-hole Camera

This is the simplest possible camera which you may have encountered in GCSE Physics and is a good approximation for many lens-based cameras. Look at Fig.3.1 showing a top view of a camera. Rays (green) from the red object pass through the camera iris (pin-hole) and form an image on the charge-coupled-device (CCD) retina. Sizes and distances are shown. The variable x is what we observe from the camera (and our code will report this). We need to know how to deduce the distance L of the object from the camera. We certainly do not know the value of d and we would like not to have to measure the width W directly.

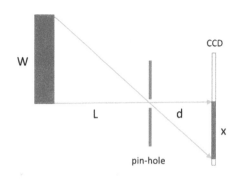

Figure 3.1 Pin-hole camera viewed from the top. Rays from the red object (width W) pass through the pinhole and create an image of size x on the camera's CCD retina.

But let's first remind ourselves of the geometry. Using similar triangles, we have

$$\frac{x}{d} = \frac{W}{L}$$

therefore

$$L = \left(\frac{Wd}{x}\right) \qquad (1)$$

This tells us that if we measure a small image width x then the object is far from the camera. Now, let's say we place an object at a known distance L_0 from the camera, and we measure the corresponding image size x_0, then substituting into (1) we have

$$L_0 = \left(\frac{Wd}{x_0}\right) \qquad (2)$$

and dividing (1) by (2) we find

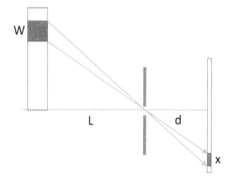

Figure 3.2 Arrangement we shall use in the lab, where the geometrical discussion is still valid.

$$L = \frac{1}{x}(L_0 x_0) \qquad (3)$$

This is useful, since the quantities in the bracket are known (we measure them), so we can deduce any distance L from the image width x, returned by our code. This is the process of *calibrating* our camera, preparing it for use. Note the units of the variables in (3). Both L and L_0 are measured in *physical* units (e.g. mm) but the x values are measured in pixels.

A Worked Example

Suppose we calibrate the camera. Assume the camera width resolution is 320 pixels. We choose to place the object so that its image completely fills the camera width. Let's assume we find this occurs at an object distance of 100 mm Then the above expression becomes

$$L = 32{,}000\,\frac{1}{x} \qquad (4)$$

Now we make a measurement of the image width x and we find this is 160 pixels. The distance to the object is $(32{,}000/160) = 200$ mm.

Now let's move the object and measure the image width x again, and say it has increased by the smallest amount, 1 pixel from 160 to 161. The object width is now $(32{,}000/161) = 198.75$ mm. This gives us the smallest measurable change in object distance for this situation, 1.25mm. Now let's investigate this, mathematically.

Sensitivity

It is useful to ask the question "how much does x change, when the distance to the object L changes?". This is one useful measure of the camera sensitivity. The quantity we wish to obtain is the relative (or fractional) change in x *to L* in other words

$$\frac{\Delta x}{\Delta L}$$

From expression (3) simple calculus tells us that

$$\frac{\Delta x}{\Delta L} = -\left(\frac{L_0 x_0}{L^2}\right) \qquad (5)$$

So, the sensitivity depends on L (in the denominator). For small values of L this sensitivity is large; a change in object distance will produce a larger Δx in the image width. This tells us that the camera is more sensitive to changes in object position L when the object is closer to the camera.

We can invert expression (4) and ask, "what is the smallest change in object distance which we can record in the camera image?".

$$\frac{\Delta L}{\Delta x} = -\frac{1}{x^2}(L_0 x_0) \qquad (6)$$

The smallest change in measured image width Δx=1 pixel. Using the values from our worked example above, $L_0 = 100\ mm$, x_0=320 pixels, and x=160 pixels we find

$$\Delta L = -\frac{1}{25600}(32000) = 1.25\ mm$$

This agrees with our worked example above. Perhaps this additional maths was not worth the effort.

3.4 Calibrating the Pixy2 Camera

The pinhole camera model presented above is useful in providing us with some understanding of the operation of a real camera. The actual operation of a real camera is best obtained using data from physical measurements. Here we report on calibration measurements for the Pixy2 camera, the experimental arrangement is shown in Fig.3.3 where the distance between the red object and the camera was changes (range 100 – 360 mm) and the image width in pixels measured. Since we know the relationship is inverse, see expression (3) then we plot distance versus 1/width. In other words, we are looking for the following *linear* relationship.

$$distance = m\left(\frac{1}{width}\right) + c \qquad (7)$$

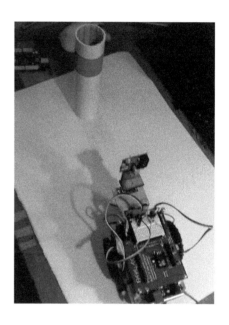

Figure 3.3 Experimental arrangement to calibrate Pixy2.

where m is the gradient of the straight line, and c is the intercept. Here's some typical results. The gradient is calculated as the length of the green arrow divided by the length of the red arrow (in units shown) and the intercept is the dist value where 1/width is zero on the plot

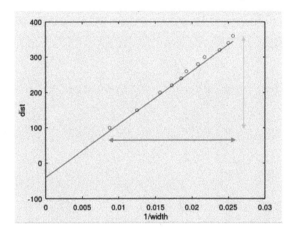

My estimates are: gradient = 15625, intercept = -40. So, the *approximate* relationship between width and distance is

$$distance = 15625 \left(\frac{1}{width}\right) - 40 \qquad (8)$$

However, we can do better than that. We can input the gradient and intercept *estimates* into a nonlinear regression program, which fits the curve to the data automatically, and gives us the optimal values for gradient and intercept.

Automatic Non-Linear fitting

This was done using the Octave script **PixyDist.m** which makes use of the function **nlinfit**. You need to provide a data set and a model to this function, here our model is the inverse relation between width and distance. The syntax for the model is

$$@(p,w) \ (p(1)./w) + p(2) \qquad (9)$$

The @(p,w) tells us that a function of variable **w** will follow where **p** are the parameters to be fit by the function. Running the script yields the following output

estimated parameters	15276.4
	-38.3
95% confidence intervals	14606.6 to 15946.1
	-51.5 to -25.1
r2 value	0.9966

The r2 value tells us that 99.7% of the data is explained by the fitted curve. The confidence intervals are fine, though the range for the second parameter is perhaps a little large. Our manual fit was not bad at all! The final relationship between width (pixels) and distance (mm) is therefore

$$dist = \frac{15276.7}{width} - 38.3 \qquad (10)$$

We can use expression (10) in our code. Just for completeness, here's the non-linear fit curve.

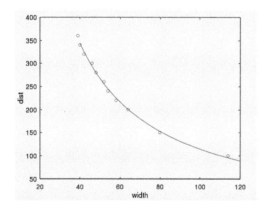

This non-linear curve fitting is a useful skill to have for other work. Now we can use the above values and write a function to convert image width to distance.

```
float getDistanceFromObject(uint16_t width) {
   float dist;
   dist = gradient/(float)width + intercept;
   return dist;
}
```

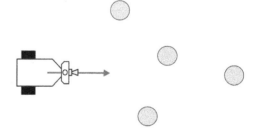

Figure 3.4 Robot moving through a cluttered environment, needs to localize each object so it can navigate between them.

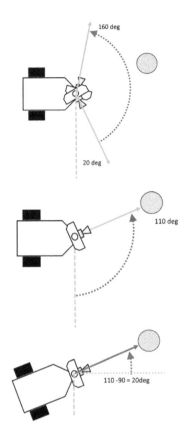

Figure 3.5 Robot scanning an environment. Top, scans, middle, finds an object at 110 degrees, bottom rotates to face the object ready for the kill

We have managed to write a computational function which captures the workings of the camera based on experimental data.

3.5 Application – Object Localization

Object *localization* is more than object *detection*. In a detection situation, we are content with detecting that the robot is about to collide with something, so we can avoid it. Localization is more precise; when a robot *localizes* an object it finds out where it is (relative to its own location), in other words, it must find the angle of the object and the distance to the object.

When a robot moves in a cluttered environment (Fig.3.4) it needs to know where the objects are located. How it does this depends on its sensors. If it has a laser sensor, which sends out a **ray** which collides with an object, then it is clear that it needs to *scan* the space it is moving into. This means rotating the laser ray from 0 to 180 degrees (looking forward) and sensing any object at any angle. This is shown in Fig. 3.5.

But when the robot has a camera, it may not need to do this scanning, since the camera captures objects within its *field of view*. The robot could simply analyse what it sees and based on this it would decide how to move.

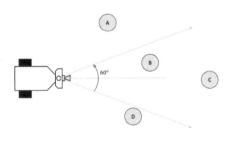

Figure 3.6 Field of view of a camera, only objects B and C are perceived

Figure 3.6 shows such a scenario. Consider the case of a single object in the camera's field of view. The Pixycam can tell us the x-location of the object (measured horizontally from the left image boundary) and we can use this to generate an *error* signal to drive the robot wheels to move the object towards the centre of the FOV. This is shown in Fig. 3.7 where the object is to the right of centre, so the robot has to rotate *clockwise* in order to centre the object

If the camera is pointing forward, then the object is in the correct place when it is at the centre of the image; here there is zero error. We define a positive error when the object is too far to the right,

$$error = x - framewidth/2$$

First, we normalize the error, dividing the above by the value of $framewidth/2$. This results in an error which is in the known range of -1.0 to 1.0 irrespective of the image frame width. The drive signal to rotate the robot is taken (in the first instance) to be proportional to this normalized error. This whole algorithm can be seen in the following code snippet.

frameWidth/2.0   X

Figure 3.7 Object to the right of centre. Its location x and frameWidth/2.0 define the error signal telling the robot how much to turn.

```
x = pixy.ccc.blocks[0].m_x;
error = ((float)x - (float)frameWidth/2.0);
error = error/((float)frameWidth/2.0);

driveR = -Kp*error;
driveL =  Kp*error;
driveServos(driveL,driveR);
```

The coefficient K_p is called the *proportional gain* for the above controller. We can estimate a suitable value. We know that the drives for our robot are around $20 - 40$, and we have normalized the error, so we find $K_p \approx 30$.

3.6 Application – Line following

Line following is a traditional robotics application where movement through a (more-or-less) static environment is required, such as a warehouse. Traditional methods use downward-facing beams of infra-red or laser light; the different intensities of light reflected from the black guiding line and the lighter surroundings is used to create an 'error' signal, which drives the robot onto the line. Some approaches use wires or magnets embedded into the floor. Of course, other approaches exist which are more suitable for dynamic environments such as lidar or full-vision which look for clear routes between obstacles in order to navigate to the robot goal.

Vision can be usefully applied to line following, since it is straightforward to design a robust line-following algorithm, and this may be supplemented with QR codes to let the robot know its exact location.

The approach to correction the robot is identical to the 'Object Localization' section presented above, except the PixyCam is set into "line" detection mode. Fig. 3.8 shows the line 'seen' by the camera, visualized using Pixymon.

Figure 3.8 Curved line seen by PixyCam which returns the end points of the vector shown.

The API returns the coordinates of the vector end points (x_0, y_0), the tail and (x_1, y_1), the head. We wish to extract information from these four numbers to compute an error signal as shown in Fig. 3.9. Looking back at Fig. 3.8 it seems reasonable to use the x-coordinate of the arrow tail to compute the error signal.

Here is some typical code which can do this. Note the similarity to the code presented in the section 'Object Localization'.

```
// Change to line-tracking
pixy.changeProg("line");

// get the lines detected
pixy.line.getAllFeatures();

// use the x-location of the tail
x0 = pixy.line.vectors[0].m_x0;
error = ((float)x - (float)frameWidth/2.0);
error = error/((float)frameWidth/2.0);

driveR = -Kp*error;
driveL =  Kp*error;
driveServos(driveL,driveR);
```

Figure 3.9 Calculation of the error from the yellow line to the centre of the image frame (dotted blue)

Note how the error is normalized (dividing by half the frameWidth), so it lies in the known range -1.0 to +1.0.

3.7 Visual Targets

Since vision is able to present a more holistic view on a scene, this can be capitalized, e.g., through the use of visual targets. One approach is not to process natural images, but to augment reality with binary images such as shown in Fig.3.10. Such images have very interesting properties; since they are planar, their orientation may be recovered when they are viewed obliquely in 3D. They will then appear trapezoidal, and the angle of the containing plane to the camera can be easily calculated. Some systems such as 'ARToolKit' use images which are both machine and human readable, others such as

Figure 3.10 Selection of Binary Acquisition Targets

ARTag are optimized for machine vision using an error-correction code. There is redundant information, so the 6x6 binary pattern of 36 bits yields 10 bits of information. The PixyCam system can recognize 16 different bar-codes, but does not recognize these unless they are in a correct orientation.

3.8 Other Approaches

There are many other established approaches and those being actively researched, but these fall out of the scope of this study. Nevertheless, it may be interesting to provide a brief overview of some of these. There is a basic problem with the use of vision in robotics; it collapses a 3D world onto a 2D retina image which then must be processed. Many algorithms exist to partially re-create features of the 3D scene. These tend to use several images of the scene, perhaps with different viewpoints, different times (depth from motion) or depth from camera focus.

Stereo Vision

The problem here, given two images of a scene from slightly different viewpoints, is to identify corresponding features in each image. Once this is done, then depth can be computed. Typically, a pre-processing stage is performed; the images are first smoothed to reduce noise, then an edge-detector (such as a Laplacian) is applied. The resulting edge features in the image pair are then matched.

Optical Flow

It is often useful to know where objects are moving in the robot's camera's field of view. Optical flow processing achieves this by comparing images from a single camera over time; differences between a time-series of images can produce a 'flow' which captures motion in the entire scene. It's a similar situation to stereo vision, corresponding features in two or more images need to be matched. Most approaches try to match patches of image pixels, though discontinuities such as corners (discovered by edge-detectors, and a bit of thought) are also useful.

Chapter 4
Wind Turbine Technology

4.1 A brief Introduction

If you take a look at the 'Live Status' of the UK National Grid at the link here,[1] you will find some interesting facts about our energy demand and generation at this moment in time. Almost half of our current production comes from gas, a respectable third from nuclear and around one sixth from wind. This division may reflect our history of energy technologies (from which we cannot escape). Renewables are currently being highlighted in the media and academic journal publications.

We shall explore two technologies: Wind Energy and Vibration Energy Harvesting (VEH). The former is now well established, you know what this is, you have seen wind turbines. There is still much research to be done, to increase their efficiency of energy production. This means increasing their physical size, which requires understanding of the tower and blade mechanics; as their designs get larger, the blade and tower structures start to flex.

Fig.4.1 is a graphic from NREL[2]s recent newsletter showing the evolution of wind turbine sizes and heights. You may like to consider where a football pitch lies on this scale. Wind energy is the fastest growing energy solution in the world, with an associated demand in engineers and researchers in the field.

---

[1] https://grid.iamkate.com/
[2] https://www.nrel.gov/wind/ National Renewable Energy Laboratory. Part of the U.S. Department of Energy.

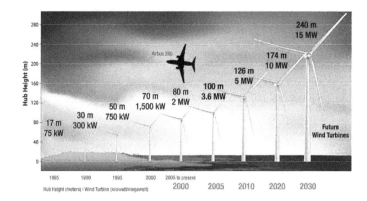

Figure 4.1 Evolution of wind turbine sizes, heights and power production. Illustration by Josh Bauer, NREL.

This chapter is about wind turbines. We shall explore three aspects of wind energy. First how a single turbine works to extract energy from the wind optimally. This is no simple task since wind-speeds do vary quite a lot. Second, we shall look at the turbulence created in the wake of a wind turbine and the effect this has on downstream turbines. Finally, we shall consider the design of Wind Farms; how the placement of each turbine within a farm can be decided to optimize something (like energy produced). All references will be to actual turbines and farms, both commercial and research.

VEHs are very new, in a research stage; they are destined to capture energy from 'things that move'. Think of a shock absorber component of your car suspension; this damps vibration by extracting it and dissipating it as heat. Bad. So, let's replace the shock absorber with a small generator, to capture the motion and charge a battery. Good. Where else could we do this? Put a VEH into our shoes, or under a train track; when a train rumbles along it depresses track segments, so let's convert this depression to electricity. VEHs will be the subject of a separate chapter.

4.2 A Philosophical Aside

Before we dive into the topic, let's just consider the *notion* of 'Renewable Energy' which may be loosely defined as 'energy that is replenished on a human timescale' (aka your lifetime), and takes on the form of sunlight, wind, hydroelectric, geothermal and others. The implication is that it will be a permanent resource, it is somehow renewed or replaced, and over time it will not diminish. Of course, that is simply nonsense, but there is something more worrying than simple nonsense.

Think about the wind turbines (renewable energy). They remove energy from the local wind system which is part of the global wind system which is a part of our climate. Change the Jet Stream and reap the consequences. Therefore, wind turbines directly affect our climate, they cause climate change, just like burning fossil fuels, but someone forgot to model and simulate this change.

4.3 Wind Energy Modelling and Simulation

In this chapter we shall explore wind energy through a number of lenses. First, we shall look at a single wind turbine and how it is controlled to maximize energy produced as wind speed changes. Second, we shall consider the fluid flow around the turbine, how the fluid downstream from the turbine is turbulent, and may influence downstream turbines. Third, we shall look at wind farms and how turbine placement can optimize energy production, based on our above results. But I told you that already.

4.4 Wind Turbine Basics

Here we take an overview of the structure and operation of a wind turbine. Several mathematical expressions will be presented; these are the ones we need to understand how to code a sophisticated simulation. The explanations of these expressions will be presented at the end of this chapter for the interested reader. First, we need to know some facts about how a wind turbine absorbs power from the wind.

The wind has a certain velocity $v(t)$ which depends on time (hence the brackets showing it is a function of time). There is another important velocity, that of the tip of the turbine blades as they rotate. If the blades have radius R and rotate with angular velocity ω radians per second, then the tip has a speed in metres per second given by

$$v = R\omega \qquad (1)$$

There is a very important quantity called the 'tip-speed ratio' which is the ratio of the tip speed to the wind speed,

$$\lambda = \frac{R\omega}{v} \qquad (2)$$

It turns out that this quantity has an optimal value (not too small, not too large) when the turbine extracts the maximum power for any given wind speed v. This ratio is about 4. If the turbine rotates too slowly (the ratio is less than 4) then it lets too much wind to pass through it uncaptured. If the turbine rotates too quickly (the ratio is greater than 4) then it appears to the wind as a solid flat disc which creates a large amount of drag. So, there is an optimal value.

Now, the power available in wind with velocity v turns out to be

$$P_{wind} = \frac{1}{2}\rho A v^3 \qquad (3)$$

where A is the area swept out by the rotor blades, and ρ is the density of air at the height where the turbine is located. This expression makes sense. However, a turbine can never extract this amount of power. If it did, then the air would come to a stop after passing through the turbine. This cannot be true, since it would prevent any more air from passing through the turbine. As we shall see, the maximum amount of power is around 59% (0.59) of the above power; this is the 'Betz' limit. But real turbines can only approach this theoretical limit, and how much they actually extract is dependent on the blade design.

Each turbine is characterized by a *power coefficient* C_p which is the ratio of power captured by the turbine to the power in the wind,

$$C_p = \frac{P_{extracted}}{P_{wind}} \qquad (4)$$

This coefficient will be less than 0.59 which is the Betz limit. Typical values for modern wind turbines are in the range of 0.47-0.50 which means they extract about 50% of the available wind energy. So, there is still some wind left over to blow smoke away from fossil-fuel fires. It turns out that the power coefficient C_p depends on the tip-speed ratio λ and also on the *blade pitch* β. So, you will see this expressed as $C_p(\lambda, \beta)$.

Let's look at how C_p depends on tip-speed ratio λ for pitch $\beta = 0$, (we'll look at the *blade pitch* β dependence later). Here's a plot made from an analytical solution. You can see that the peak of C_p at 0.479 is close to the Betz limit, and this occurs for $\lambda = 8$.

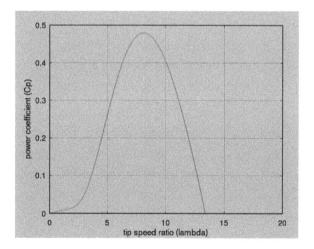

For the Seimens SWT-3.6-107 3.6MW turbines, installed on the Walney wind farm, this means a power generated of (0.479)(3.6) = 1.72MW, with the blade tip moving at 8 times the wind speed, (easy to achieve since the blade length is 54m.

Later we shall consider how to ensure that a turbine is operating optimally, at the peak of the C_p curve. But while we have the tip-speed ratio in mind, let's prepare some ground. Let's say this ratio is optimal at 8, then the wind speed drops. From equation (2) we see the ratio increases, so it is too large. To reduce it we must reduce ω, the speed of rotation of the turbine.

Power Output Curves

The $C_p - \lambda$ curve is fundamental in understanding the details of wind turbine control (below), but it is somewhat unintuitive since λ conflates two variables, wind speed v and turbine rotational velocity ω. Using the expressions (2), (3), (4) we can derive expressions for the power output in terms of ω or v.

$$P_{turbine} = \frac{1}{2}\rho\pi R^5 C_p(\lambda, \beta)\omega^3 \quad (5a)$$

$$P_{turbine} = \frac{1}{2}\rho\pi R^2 C_p(\lambda, \beta)v^3 \quad (5b)$$

Expression (5a) lets us plot out the turbine power as a function of rotor speed, for various wind speeds. So, we have separated out both parts of λ. Curves are plotted for windspeeds of 9, 11, 13, and 15 m/s.

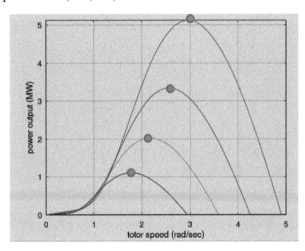

For each wind speed, there is a particular rotor speed where the power extracted is maximum, as shown by the red dots. This, of course, produces the optimal tip-speed ratio. Join the dots and you'll get the 'maximum power point tracking (MMPT) of the turbine; the turbine is controlled (by varying its speed of rotation) so it stays on this curve as the wind speed varies.

4.5 Structure of a Wind Turbine

You have all seen the main components of a Wind Turbine; the tower, the rotor and the nacelle (which houses a gearbox and generator).

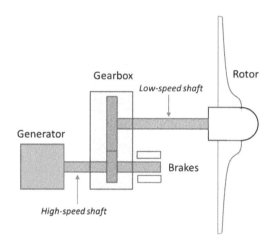

First we need to understand why there is a gearbox. The generator is ultimately connected to the grid which supplies alternating current at a frequency of 50Hz (cycles per second). The turbine *must* emit current with this frequency, it must synchronise with the grid, otherwise the grid would pull the turbine generator into synch and to do this would apply a huge mechanical load which would lead to failure.

If the generator had one pole producing current, then at 50Hz the generator would need to turn at 3000 rpm. This is much faster than the turbine blades rotate, so there must be a gearbox to convert slow blade rotation to the higher generator

Figure 4.2 NREL CART3 Turbine. Photo by Lee Jay Fingersh NREL 54232

speed. For the NREL CART3 turbine the gearbox ratio is 43.2.

There are two main types of turbine: fixed-speed and variable speed. Fixed-speed devices are connected directly to the grid with the generator rotating at the required 3000 rpm. It turns out that if you let the turbine rotate with a variable speed, then it can get an extra 2.5% power out of the wind. Of course, it cannot be directly connected to the grid; another layer of power electronics is required to do the frequency synchronization. We shall be working with variable speed turbines

4.6 Regions of Operation

There are four regions of operation for a variable-speed turbine shown in the graph below for the CART3 turbine (see Fig 4.2) which we shall be modelling.

In Region 1 there is not enough power in the wind to offset turbine mechanical losses, so the turbine does not rotate. In Region 2 the turbine is operating below its rated power, here 600 kW and it speed increases with wind speed. In Region 3 the turbine is operating at its rated power, so its speed of rotation is held constant even though the wind speed may increase.

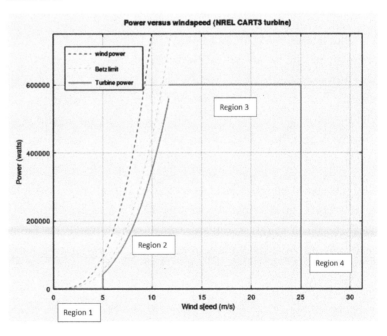

Finally in Region 4, the wind speed is too high for the turbine controller to hold it at the rated power, so the turbine shuts down.

Now we turn to discussing the turbine *controller*, systems that maintain the turbine at the desired operating point. There are different approaches to control in Region 2 and Region 3 as we shall see.

4.7 Region 2 Controller

We need to control the turbine speed of rotation; this is represented by the maths symbol ω (omega) and has units of radians per second. For a turbine rotating at one rev per second, then the angular speed is $\omega = 2\pi$ which is around 6 radians per second. The rated speed of the CART-3 turbine (in Region 3) is $\omega_{rated} = 4.367$ radians per second, so it's rotating less than once per second.

To understand how to control ω we must ask ourselves what is *causing* ω, or more specifically what is *causing* ω *to change*? Well one thing is the wind, and when this passes through the blades it exerts a *torque* on the blades causing ω the angular speed to increase. The symbol for torque is τ (tau, pronounced like cow) so if τ_{wind} is the torque on the turbine due to wind, then the rotation velocity changes like this

$$\frac{d\omega}{dt} = \frac{1}{J}\tau_{wind} \qquad (6)$$

The left-hand side is saying omega is changing with time, and the right-hand side is saying that the torque from the wind is causing this change. Also, since the right-hand side is positive, then the wind torque is making the turbine speed up. The symbol J is the inertia of the turbine, playing the role of mass, more inertia means smaller rate of change of omega. So the wind makes the rotor speed up, and therefore we need something to apply torque in the opposite direction to prevent the turbine running away. The *generator* is the perfect candidate, and if τ_{gen} is the turbine generator we can complete the above expression for the change in rotation velocity

$$\frac{d\omega}{dt} = \frac{1}{J}\left(\tau_{wind} - \tau_{gen}\right) \qquad (7)$$

So, we see the generator is a crucial part of a wind turbine, as well as generating electricity, it can act as a controller to fix omega. You can see from the above expression that when the generator matches its torque to the torque from the blades, then $\tau_{wind} - \tau_{gen} = 0$ so the rate of change of omega is zero; the turbine's speed does not change.

Now we have to add in some details. First, we introduce an expression for the torque from the wind (this will be derived in an appendix).

$$\tau_{wind} = \frac{1}{2}\rho\pi R^5 \frac{C(\lambda, \beta)}{\lambda^3}\omega^2 \qquad (8)$$

This looks formidable, but perhaps you can see the blade area πr^2 lurking there, and the only true variable on the right is omega, the rotation speed. So, this expression links aerodynamic torque and wind speed.

The simplest way to model generator-based control is to make the generator torque depend on omega in the same way, so we choose

$$\tau_{gen} = \frac{1}{2}\rho\pi R^5 K\omega^2 \qquad (9)$$

Where we need to choose a value for the constant K. Plugging (8) and (9) into (7) we find

$$\frac{d\omega}{dt} = \frac{1}{2J}\rho\pi R^5 \omega^2 \left(\frac{C(\lambda, \beta)}{\lambda^3} - K\right) \qquad (10)$$

Now here comes the magic; the choice of K. Remember we want the turbine to change its speed, so it is operating at the peak of the C_p curve. Then its speed does not change so $d\omega/dt = 0$. So, we choose K as follows

$$K = \frac{C_{pMax}}{\lambda_{opt}^3} \qquad (11)$$

Now expression (10) becomes

$$\frac{d\omega}{dt} = \frac{1}{2J} \rho \pi R^5 \omega^2 \left(\frac{C(\lambda, \beta)}{\lambda^3} - \frac{C_{pMax}}{\lambda_{opt}^3} \right) \qquad (12)$$

So, when we are operating at the peak of the C_p curve, we have $C_p = C_{pMax}$ and $\lambda^3 = \lambda_{opt}^3$ so the expression in the brackets is zero and the turbine speed does not change.

We can see what happens, for a given wind speed if the turbine it is turning too fast (omega too large) Since $\lambda = \omega R/v$ then we have $\lambda > \lambda_{opt}$ so, the first bracketed term in (12) is smaller than the second so the bracket is negative, so the turbine slows down. Conversely if the turbine is turning too slowly then $\lambda < \lambda_{opt}$ so the first term in (12) becomes larger than the second, the bracket is positive, so the turbine speeds up.

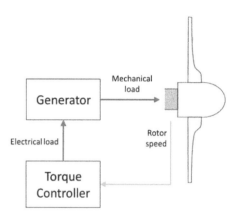

Figure 4.3 Region 2 Control Loop. Rotor speed is measured, then the controller changes the electrical load on the generator which changes the mechanical load (torque) on the turbine shaft.

You may feel you have lost sight of what is actually changing to effect the control. Well, this is the generator torque, expression (9) with the value of K from (11). So, the electrical load on the generator is changed depending on the rotational speed of the turbine. The electrical load determines the generator torque. Stated simply, if the turbine is rotating too fast then the generator load is increased to slow it down and *vice-versa*.

For the more mathematically inclined we can explain how the controller works by looking again at expression (12) from which we derive the following inequalities,

$$\frac{d\omega}{dt} < 0 \qquad when \qquad C_p < \left(\frac{C_{pMax}}{\lambda_{opt}^3} \right) \lambda^3 \qquad (13)$$

$$\frac{d\omega}{dt} > 0 \qquad when \qquad C_p > \left(\frac{C_{pMax}}{\lambda_{opt}^3} \right) \lambda^3 \qquad (14)$$

which gives the condition for rotor slow-down (13) and speed-up (14). We can show this graphically, in the plot below the blue curve is just $C_p(\lambda)$, how the power coefficient varies with tip-speed ratio. and the red curve is just

$$\left(\frac{C_{pMax}}{\lambda_{opt}^3}\right)\lambda^3$$

So, when the blue curve is greater than the red curve, the turbine speeds up, and when the blue curve is less than the red curve the turbine slows down.

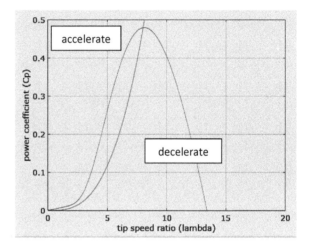

4.8 Region 3 Pitch Controller

When the turbine has reached its rated rotational speed, for CART3 this is 4.367 rad/sec, then power needs to be shed (or at least not absorbed) if the wind speed increases any further. This is done by changing the pitch β (beta) of the turbine blades, so they extract less energy from the wind. A pitch of zero degrees means the sharp edge of the blade is facing the wind, so it extracts zero power. A classical PID controller is used here, though the derivative part is not often used since this is sensitive to abrupt changes. The formulation of the controller is straightforward

$$\frac{d\beta}{dt} = K_p(\omega_{rated} - \omega) \qquad (15)$$

So, if the turbine starts rotating too fast then $\omega > \omega_{rated}$ and the right-hand side of (13) is negative so the blade pitch is decreased, so there is less of the blade 'facing' the wind. When the turbine is rotating too slow, the right-hand side is positive, so the pitch is increased, and the blades absorb more power.

Chapter 5
Wind Farms

5.1 A brief Introduction

The key to understanding how to design successful wind farms centres on understanding the wake produced behind a single turbine, and how this interacts with downwind turbines. The complexity of the wake structure over a complete wind farm is shown in the photo below for the 'Horns Rev II' farm.

Photo by: Bel Air Aviation Denmark – Helicopter Services. January 26th, 2016.

You can see a wake of vortices produced by each turbine and that some downwind turbines lay in the wake of upwind turbines. As we shall see this air turbulence has both positive and negative effects. It allows *mixing* of the slower air immediately behind the turbine rotor with surrounding faster air. This allows the wind to 'recover' speed in the wake at large distances from the turbine. So, while a turbine downstream does not experience the full windspeed, it experiences a speed quite close to it. So that's a good effect of turbulence. A bad effect is that turbulence can cause large mechanical loads on downwind turbines as the quasi-periodic vortices impact on downwind rotors. Now let's consider this mixing effect.

5.2 The Single Wake

Mixing of Air

To understand how the wind speed varies along a single wake, we need to see how wind is mixed. This is shown in the diagram below.

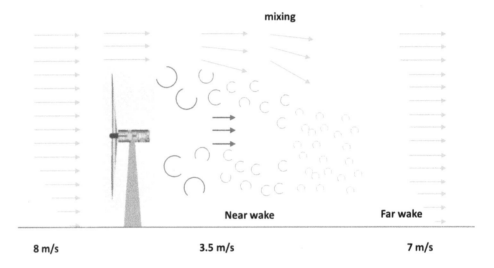

The wind enters from the left (8 m/s), and immediately behind the turbine blade a system of vortices is created. This is a region of low wind speed (3 m/s, red arrows). So, the wind speed drops dramatically as the wind traverses the turbine rotor. Then the shed vortices travel downstream, and their circulation starts to dissipate. Also, wind (at full speed) which has not crossed the turbine starts to mix in with the vortices and so the wind speed in the wake starts to increase.

There are two regions to the wake; in the *near wake* the wind speed is low (since the turbine has extracted energy). This region occupies several rotor diameters. In the *far wake* the mixing is complete and the wind velocity has increased (7 m/s – blue arrows). This gives some hints at where not to place a turbine downwind; the near wake region must be avoided.

The Jensen Model

This is the earliest (1983) and simplest model of wake expansion but is still used in software today (including Floris). Its purpose was to increase the efficiency of wind farms by locating turbines to avoid wake losses.

The model assumes that the wake diameter starts with the value of the turbine diameter and expands linearly with distance from the turbine. It completely neglects the near wake, so is based on a progressive mixing of the slow wind behind the turbine disk with the fast wind outside this disc. This is shown in the diagram below

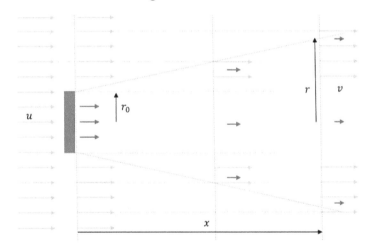

The blue arrows show the wind starting with speed u on the left. The reduced wind speed after the turbine u_R is shown by the shorter red arrows, as the wake spreads linearly these are diluted as faster wind mixes in from outside the cylinder around the turbine. The speed at the right is v.

The expression for the velocity at the right (derived in the appendix) is

$$v = u\left[1 - 2a\left(\frac{r_0}{r_0 + \alpha x}\right)^2\right] \qquad (1)$$

with

$$a = \frac{1}{2}\left(1 - \frac{u_R}{u}\right) \qquad (2)$$

where u_R is the wind speed immediately after the rotor (to its right). This constant expresses the *velocity deficit* caused by the turbine. For a free wind speed of 8 m/s and a typical $u_R = $ 4 m/s the velocity deficit is 0.25. It's just an indication of the effect of the turbine on the wind velocity near the turbine.

The parameter α determines how quickly the wave expands with distance from the turbine, whether the cone is more or less pointed. This is an empirical parameter which is about 0.075 for on-shore or 0.04 for off-shore. This means that on-shore wakes tend to spread wider.

Figure 5.1 shows a plot of expression (1). The deficit across the rotor is shown (not part of the expression) the speed dropping from 8 m/s to around 4m/s. Moving down the wake you can see how the speed is rising slowly ending up around 7 m/s at a distance 1200 metres (1.2 km) from the turbine.

The bottom image shows the output from Floris; here red is 8 m/s and blue around 4 m/s. This shows how the Jensen wake develops in 2D, and you can see the wind speed increasing in the wake.

5.3 Interacting Wakes

Two Turbines with Lateral Displacement

This is the starting point to understand wind turbine placement in farms, where a second turbine is place wholly in the wake of the lead turbine. Two scenarios are shown in the figure below. The first shows the second turbine placed at a separation of 1.2 km. The powers produced by each

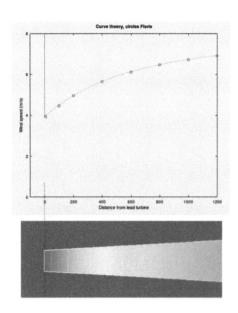

Figure 5.1 Top: plot of expression (1). Bottom: corresponding field from Floris

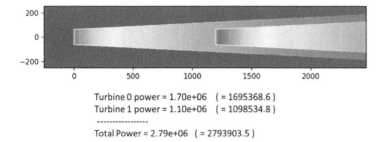

Turbine 0 power = 1.70e+06   (= 1695368.6)
Turbine 1 power = 1.10e+06   (= 1098534.8)

Total Power = 2.79e+06   (= 2793903.5)

turbine are shown. The second turbine is producing less power since it is receiving wind at a lower speed; Floris tells us this is 6.92 m/s. That's a consequence of being in the wake. If we increase the separation, then we shall increase the power generated by the second turbine shown below for a separation of 1.8 km. This is a consequence of more free wind mixing in.

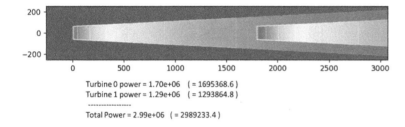

Turbine 0 power = 1.70e+06   (= 1695368.6)
Turbine 1 power = 1.29e+06   (= 1293864.8)

Total Power = 2.99e+06   (= 2989233.4)

Here the wind in front of the turbine is now 7.3 m/s due to the wake expansion and free wind at 8 m/s mixing in, as discussed above.

> We can do a nice little calculation at this point. Since we know that power is proportional to wind velocity *cubed* then the ratios calculated here should be the same
>
> $$\left(\frac{7.3}{6.92}\right)^3 = 1.174 \qquad \frac{1.29}{1.10} = 1.173$$

Two Turbines with Wake Steering

Wake steering is a promising area of wind farm research. The idea is to angle the lead turbine by changing its yaw so that its wake is partially deflected from the downwind turbine. The idea is shown in the Floris image below

The baseline case without wake steering produces a total power of 4.55 MW, and with wake (yaw = 20 degs) steering this is increased to 4.83 MW, just over 6%. This is a huge increase which is obtained for no additional capital cost.

How wake steering works is relatively straightforward to understand. Due to the deflection of the lead turbine wake, the second turbine is receiving wind from outside the wake.

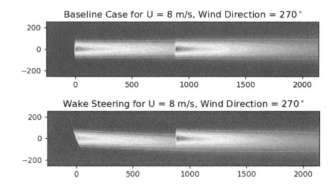

The average speed received by the second turbine has increased, you can clearly see this in the above figure. It is interesting to see that the wake is steered in the opposite direction to the yaw angle. This is a consequence of resolving the turbine thrust into directions parallel and orthogonal to the wind direction. Material for an appendix.

A Column of Several Turbines

If you search for wind farm layouts, you will find that many are composed of repeated columns of turbines. Therefore, it makes sense to study a column as shown in the graphic below.

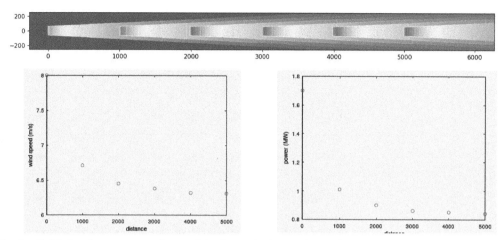

The Floris field is shown together with the windspeeds and individual turbine powers at each location. The results are interesting. Of course, we expect turbines further downwind to produce less power, and they do! But the decrease in wind speed and power slows down after the first two or three turbines, and both tend to asymptotic values. The wind speed tends to just under 6.5 m/s and the power to just above 0.8 MW. So, this suggests that it is very reasonable to build long columns of turbines.

Changing the Layout

One approach to designing a 2D windfarm is to start with a 1D scenario, and to 'morph' this into 2D. For example, we could take the 6-turbine column and displace every other turbine sideways to create two columns of 3 turbines. We could calculate how the power changes as a function of how much we displace the turbines.

But first we need to understand the effect of changing the inter-turbine separation on the total power generated. This can be done by running several Floris computations. The results of such a calculation are shown in Fig. 5.2. As expected, the power increases with separation, since more free wind speed is available to all turbines as it mixes into the wakes. But the rate of improvement slows down, and, once more, we seem to be heading for an asymptote. Of course, increasing separation comes with a cost; the cost of the cables

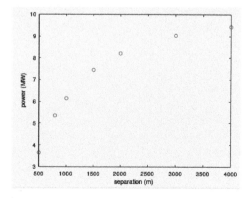

Figure 5.2 Power produced by a column of 6 turbines as a function of their separation.

connecting the turbines to the electricity sub-station. This sounds like the beginning of an optimization problem.

Turning now to morphing the 6-turbine column into two adjacent columns of 3 turbines, we find a very interesting result as the separation between the columns ('offset') is increased. This is shown in Fig. 5.3. As we start to increase the offset from zero there is initially no increase in power until the separation is between 80 and 90 m. Then there is a sudden increase in power with separation until we reach around 150m or so, after which the power remains pretty constant.

Such a plot is indicative of a *binary* situation, where we change from one behaviour or arrangement to another. You may have seen such a plot in the study of binary electronic circuits. I feel sure you can work out what is going on here, it would be a shame to give you the answer just now.

5.4 Layout Optimization

This is a very complex topic, there are many algorithms available. Here we shall restrict the discussion to the technique available in Floris.

The whole idea centres on 'constrained optimization. Let's take these two words separately. Optimization means changing the position of the turbines in a farm to achieve the maximum Annual Energy Production (AEP). Constrained means we have some constraints on the problem, for example the turbines must be located within a given boundary, and there may be some places where turbines may not be located, e.g., in a school playground. So, optimization and constraints need to be taken together.

Floris provides us with a range of problem solvers, e.g., the AEP given frequencies of wind speeds and direction subject to the constraints of a given boundary and minimum distance between the turbines. In addition, constraints on the turbine heights may be supplied, and optimization may be made on the Cost of Energy (COE) rather than the AEP.

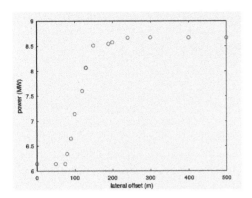

Figure 5.3 Power as a function of offset between two columns of three turbine starting from 0 (all turbines in a row)

The example shown below was computed using Floris, to optimize the turbine layout to maximize the AEP. Wind speed and direction were provided, and boundary constraints asserted.

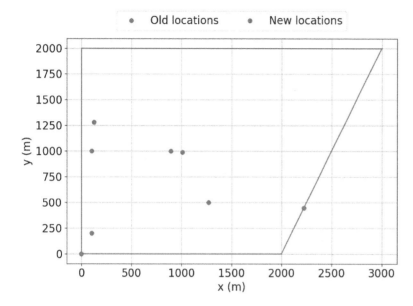

The total gain in AEP due to the optimization was 3.0%.

The actual optimization routine used the 'sequential quadratic programming' algorithm; the maths behind this is really beyond this course.

5.5 Appendix Material

Derivation of Power and Torque and Betz Limit

Let's have a look at wind passing a single turbine. The diagram below shows air passing through a stream-tube, all the air remains in that tube and we are not yet considering mixing.

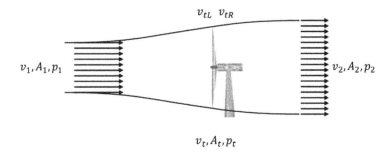

The parameters are air velocity, pressure and area of the stream tube upwind, at the turbine rotor and downwind. Arrows show that the wind speed is decreasing as can be understood from the diagram below

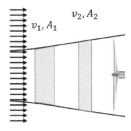

The blue areas show a given element of volume as it moves through the tube. Assuming air is incompressible then the volume stays the same. Therefore, the length of the element must get smaller since the area gets larger. So, we have for the volumes

$$\Delta l_1 A_1 = \Delta l_2 A_2 \qquad (A1)$$

But the above snapshot shows movement over the same time interval so dividing the above by this interval we find how the volume changes with time

$$\frac{\Delta l_1}{\Delta t} A_1 = \frac{\Delta l_2}{\Delta t} A_2 = v_1 A_1 = v_2 A_2 \quad (A2)$$

So we see that the air slows down. Multiplying by the air density ρ we get an expression for the rate of change of mass (the same at all places)

$$\frac{\Delta m}{\Delta t} = \rho A_1 v_1 = \rho A_t v_t = \rho A_2 v_2 \quad (A3)$$

Hence the rate of change in momentum of the air stream between when it enters and when it leaves the stream-tube is

$$\frac{\Delta m}{\Delta t} v_1 - \frac{\Delta m}{\Delta t} v_2 = \rho A_t v_t (v_1 - v_2) \quad (A4)$$

and this is caused by the thrust on the turbine disc. We can use Bernoulli on in the stream-tube at the left and right sides of the turbine disc

$$p_1 + \tfrac{1}{2}\rho v_1^2 = p_{tL} + \tfrac{1}{2}\rho v_{tL}^2 \quad (A5a)$$

$$p_{tR} + \tfrac{1}{2}\rho v_{tR}^2 = p_2 + \tfrac{1}{2}\rho v_2^2 \quad (A5b)$$

Assuming that $p_1 = p_2$ and $V_{tL} = V_{tR}$ then the pressure difference across the disc is

$$p_{tL} - p_{tR} = \tfrac{1}{2}\rho (v_1^2 - v_2^2) \quad (A6)$$

Since force is pressure times area, we can use this to get another expression for force on the disc

$$F = \tfrac{1}{2}\rho (v_1^2 - v_2^2) A_t \quad (A7)$$

Equating the two expressions for force we find

$$\rho A_t v_t (v_1 - v_2) = \tfrac{1}{2}\rho (v_1^2 - v_2^2) A_t$$

$$v_t = \tfrac{1}{2}(v_1 + v_2) \quad (A8)$$

which tells us the windspeed at the turbine is the average of the upwind and downwind wind speeds.

Finally, we have an expression for the power delivered to the turbine. Power is force x velocity, so at the turbine we find

$$P = F_t v_t = 2\rho A_t v_t^2 (v_1 - v_t) \qquad (A9)$$

This is an interesting expression which shows how the power depends on the wind speed near the turbine. There are two factors, v_t^3 which increases with v_t and $(v_1 - v_t)$ which decreases with v_t, so we expect the power - v_t curve to have a peak which it does. To find the peak we proceed as usual,

$$\frac{\partial P}{\partial v_t} = 0,$$

which gives the result $v_t = \frac{2}{3} v_1$ and also $v_2 = \frac{1}{3} v_1$.

Finally we turn to the maximum power expression, plugging this value of v_t into the expression for power P we find

$$P_{max} = \frac{8}{27} \rho A_t v_1^3 \qquad (A10)$$

and if we define the power coefficient as

$$C_p = \frac{P}{\frac{1}{2} \rho A_t v_1^3}$$

then we find

$$C_{p,max} = \frac{16}{27} = 0.593 \qquad (A11)$$

This is the maximum achievable efficiency of a wind turbine (59.3%) and is known as the Betz limit

Derivation of the Jensen Wake Expression

Here we shall derive equation (1) the wind speed variation inside a wake taking Jensen's approach assuming we are in the far-field wake where perfect mixing is occurring.

Here's a diagram which highlights the regions of air arriving at the plane on the right, a distance x from the turbine rotor

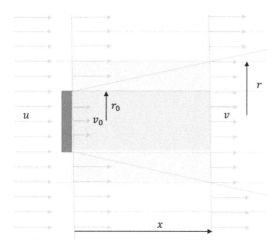

The total air arriving is the sum of the air from the red and green regions. The red is the slow air (speed just behind the rotor) and the green is the fast air (free). The respective rates of arrival of air masses are

$$\rho \pi r_o^2 v_0 \quad (red)$$

$$\rho \pi (r^2 - r_o^2) u \quad (green)$$

So we have

$$\rho \pi r_o^2 v_0 + \rho \pi (r^2 - r_o^2) u \ = \rho \pi r^2 v \quad (A12)$$

hence

$$r_o^2 v_0 + (r^2 - r_o^2) u \ = r^2 v \quad (A13)$$

Now we define

$$a = \frac{u - v_0}{u}$$

so that $v_0 = u(1 - a)$ and using (A8) we find

$$v = u(1 - 2a) \quad (A14)$$

This is correct for a situation with a near and a far wake, but Jensen ignored the near wake and used (A14) as an expression for v_0.

Substituting (A14) into (A13) leads to expression (1).

Chapter 6
Computational Fluid Dynamics

6.1 A brief Introduction

The motion of air around a wind turbine is a very complicated but interesting phenomenon. When several turbines are arranged into a wind-farm then the situation becomes even more complex. Fluid dynamics is the study of fluid (liquid and air) around one or a few objects, typically we consider air foils, cylinders and other bluff objects, and of course fish.

The motion of an element of fluid can be broken up into three parts (which can exist in combinations), this is shown in Fig.6.1 Translation is motion along a curve or streamline, when a fluid rotates it shows *vorticity* and fluid shear is caused by the fluid *viscosity* which is another word for friction. The actual behaviour of a fluid depends on its speed past an object, we expect streamlined flow without any vorticity for relatively small fluid speeds, whereas at higher speeds vortices are formed and at even higher speeds we experience a phenomenon called 'vortex shedding'. All of this will be explained below.

The maths of fluid dynamics is challenging, so we shall take a phenomenological approach here, gaining understanding from examples. One serious limitation is that our studies will be limited to 2D

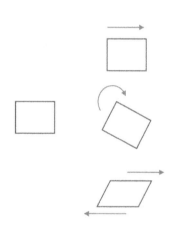

Figure 6.1 Types of fluid motion. The element on the left may translate (top), rotate (centre) and shear (bottom)

6.2 Flow past some simple shapes

Air Foil

This shape is used for aircraft wings and wind turbines, there is actually a whole family of shapes, they are designed to have a large ratio of 'lift' force, (making the aircraft fly, or the turbine rotate), to the 'drag' force (opposing the aircraft motion or pushing against the turbine.

The flow of air around an airfoil at low speeds is shown in the diagram below (computed using 'LilyPad')

The flow is symmetrical, there is little circulation of air (vorticity). At a slightly higher speed the flow changes like this where the formation of vortices is clear.

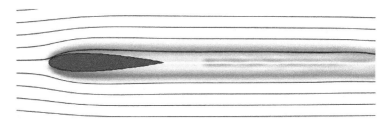

How do airfoils produce lift? There are several ways to explain this, a simple one draws on Bernoulli's principle, the faster the air, the lower its pressure. So when the wing is given a little angle of attack the speed over the top is more than under the bottom, so more pressure at the bottom, therefore lift. Another explanation draws on Newton's laws. The example below shows the airfoil at an angle 0.5 degree

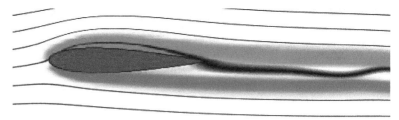

and the air leaving the airfoil has a clear downward component. The wing therefore experiences an upward lift force.

Cylinder

This is an important geometry which you find all around us, telephone and electricity cables, guy wires on bridges and antennas. At low fluid velocities there is streamlined flow around the object like this (speed 0.1)

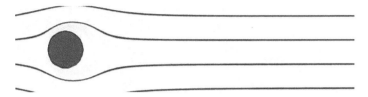

and at higher velocities (0.5) we find strong vortices, which

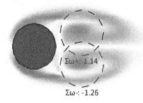

rotate in opposite directions. At higher velocities these vortices detach from the cylinder, and form a Von-Karmen 'vortex street' behind the cylinder (v = 2.5)

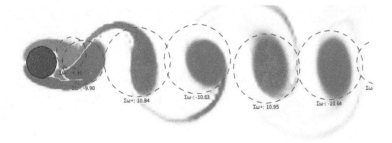

This periodic shedding of vortices poses a problem in many situations. Since the vortices are alternately shed up then down, then they will apply a periodic force to the cylinder. This will excite it into oscillation. You may have heard telephone lines howling in the wind, it's this phenomenon you are experiencing. Vortex shedding destroyed the Tacoma Narrows Bridge and the Ferrybridge cooling tower.

At higher velocities turbulence results, it's not possible to visualize this with LilyPad.

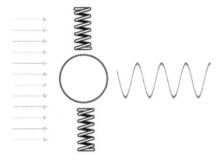

Figure 6.2 Structure of a Vibration Energy Harvester

6.3 Vibration Energy Harvesting (VEH)

Vortex shedding can be turned to use if the vibration is extracted from the cylinder. Usually, electricity is created using the piezo-electric effect, a material that produces electric charge when it is bent. The cylinder can be thought of as being suspended between two springs and will oscillate at the system's natural frequency, see Fig.6.2. Such bladeless turbines are being developed, while they may be around 25% as efficient as a conventional turbine, they may be built with a higher farm density. Current plans aim to produce power outputs of 4kW.

Much research is focused on development of microscale VEH and draw on a range of 'things that vibrate'. Replace your car shock absorbers with VEHs and charge your battery. But the biggest research interest at the moment is in VEHs which supply only milliwatts or microwatts of power. These could be used to power remote devices in the IoT age and also body-mounted monitoring devices. Yet interesting calculations appear in the literature. It is reported that about 85kW can be produced from a 70-storey building in the wind.

Chapter 7
Control Theory

7.1 A brief Introduction

Think of a central heating system where we set the thermostat to a desired temperature. A sensor in the room measures the actual temperature, and the difference between the two provides an *error* value which is sent to the heating unit which provides heat until the actual temperature rises to the desired temperature. The error is then zero, so the heating unit is turned off.

Another example is car cruise control. We set a desired speed, e.g., 30 mph and a sensor on the drivetrain measures the actual speed. Again, the difference between the two provides an error value which is sent to the motor and increases its drive. When we go down a hill, the actual speed will increase above 30 mph, so now the error signal is negative, and this reduces the motor drive.

7.2 Robot Line Following

We apply control theory to the problem of a robot following a line, shown in Fig. 7.1 which uses computer vision. The camera reports the position x0 of the line in its frame and measures the error from the desired location which is the centre of the frame. The error can be used to drive the robot wheels to turn the robot towards the line.

The question arises, how to convert the error into motor drive? We assume that the error has been *normalized* so we know it is in the range -1.0 to +1.0, or thereabouts. Now typical motors will need a *drive* signal of 10 or 20 units, so we need to bump up the error signal. Here's code we have used:

Figure 7.1 Robot line following scenario. Here the robot is too far to the right of the line and must rotate anti-clockwise

```
driveR = -Kp*error;
driveL =  Kp*error;
driveServos(driveL,driveR);
```

The coefficient **Kp** is the *proportional* coefficient, since this makes drive proportional to error. Since the error is about 1.0 and we need, say 20 drive units, we should have Kp about 20.

Here we shall start the development of the PID theory. Let's consider a toy problem where the robot has to move so that its lateral position is 1mm from the centre of the line. Let's try a few values of **Kp** to see how it fairs. Have a look at Fig.7.2 where the robot starts off at 0 mm and we drive it using the proportional error towards the 1 mm position (up the side of the graph). This is a graph of robot position against time, and we want the position to become 1.0, near the top of the graph. Horror! None of the values of **Kp** actually work! For values of 1 and 10, the robot never reaches the 1mm target position. For a larger value of 50, the robot overshoots and oscillates about a value less than 1, until the oscillations damp out.

So, making **Kp** too large will make the system *unstable* though there is one clear advantage in larger values of **Kp**, you can see from the graphs that the robot approaches the target distance *more quickly* for larger values.

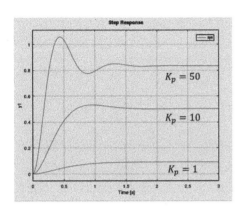

Figure 7.2 Response of robot to a disturbance for three values of Kp.

7.3 Enter the PID Controller

PID means *Proportional-Integral-Derivative* control, each of these terms form a separate calculation in the controller – you have already seen the *proportional* control. PID controllers are ubiquitous in engineering solutions, and are well-understood, though some aspects are more art than science.

The structure of the PID controller is shown in Fig.7.3 using maths symbolism. The error signal $e(t)$ comes in at the left and the computed drive exits at the right to drive out motors. The three boxes in the middle make different computations on the error signal, and these are summed (the Σ symbol) which form the final drive. We know how to calculate the proportional component. The integral component sums all the errors over time (this will include negative error values, so

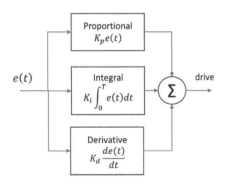

Figure 7.3 Structure of the PID controller. There are three calculations which are then summed to produce the drive.

the sum will not simply increase). The derivative component takes the *difference* between current and previous errors.

Let's see what the extra components achieve, starting with the derivative. We keep Kp = 50 (see Fig.7.2 where we had the horrible overshoot and oscillations) and look at two values of Kd; Kd = 0 and Kd = 10. You can see the results in Fig.7.4. With Kd = 0, we have oscillations and overshoot, but with Kd = 10, the oscillations are damped out, so the position rises smoothly towards the desired position 1.0. There is clearly an improvement, the robot will not display those oscillations or 'hunting' behaviour. Note also that the 'rise time', the speed at which the robot approaches the desired position is hardly influenced by the derivative component.

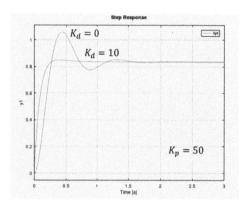

Figure 7.4 PD controller with two values of Kd

There is just one snag. The robot does not oscillate, but it does not reach the desired position of 1.0. That's the job of the *integral* part of the controller. Two values for **Ki** are shown in Fig.7.5, you can see the effect of the integral component is to move the robot closer to its desired position. In summary, here's what the components do

K_p	proportional	Larger value increases speed to goal but gives overshoot and oscillation
K_d	derivative	Overshoot and oscillation removed. But does not achieve goal
K_i	integral	Achieves goal

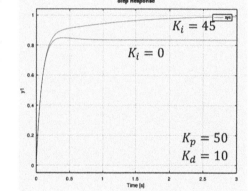

Figure 7.5 Addition of the integral component gets the robot closer to the desired position 1.0.

The Control Loop

Let's put all of this together and see where the robot fits in.

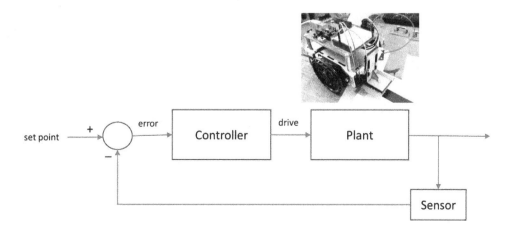

At the left is the set point, in our example the desired robot position. At the right, a sensor monitors the actual robot position and sends this back to the start of the loop. Here the difference between desired and actual position is calculated to give the error signal which is then input into the controller.

As mentioned, PID controllers are ubiquitous, the 'plant' refers to the system under control, such as our central heating or car cruise control.

The actual values of K_p, K_d, and K_i needed depend on the details of the plant and may differ between the lab robots since all of these are slightly different.

Tuning the controller.

This refers to finding the values of K_p, K_d, and K_i. This is usually done experimentally and is something of a black art which is learned by experience. The usual approach is as follows.

Stage 1.	Set all coefficients to 0
Stage 2.	Increase K_p until the robot shows signs of overshoot or oscillation
Stage 3.	Increase K_d until the oscillation disappears
Stage 4.	Increase K_i until the robot achieves the desired position. This may mean reducing K_p and perhaps K_i.

Chapter 8
Neural Circuits

8.1 A brief Introduction

This chapter on Neural Circuits is all about how the study of biological neurons inside our brains and linked to our senses and to our motor functions (arms, legs, heart etc.,) can inform how we create digital computer software and hardware artefacts. I have in mind physical artefacts such as legged robots which draw on parallels with real biological creatures, or image processing algorithms which draw on understanding of how the biological eye functions. There are many sorts of eyes, from the mammalian to the fly-eye which have different structures and purposes. There are many sorts of legged creatures (2, 4, 6, 8, lots) of legs and most of these biological creatures have been used to design physical robots.

Computers have been always linked to a study of the real world and in fact a simulation of real-world phenomena. Perhaps the earliest was the Greek Antikythera, discovered in the 20th century, but believed to be over 2000 years old. It was a mechanical device used to predict the positions of the sun, moon and planets, predict eclipses and (in retrospect) to determine the dates of ancient Olympic games.

Computers have been always linked with mathematics, and in particular solutions of 'Ordinary Differential Equations' (ODEs) which predict how things change with time, from the trajectories of wartime projectiles to the changes of stock market values, the beating of the heart and the synchronized flashing of fireflies.

Computers have always been linked with Electronic Engineering; before our digital age, in the era of analogue computers machines contained circuits; electronic adders, multipliers and integrators (which solved ODEs) all linked together with wires, where voltages represented variables, and controlled power stations, automotive control and more.

Computers have always been linked with cognitive psychology which attempts to understand how the mind works (even though no-one has proved that the mind is located in the brain). Of particular interest to me is how language comprehension and composition (story-writing) works.

Computers have always been linked with medicine, from the early stethoscopes through the development of digital radiography to contemporary functional Nuclear Magnetic Resonance imaging (f-MRI).

You get the idea. Computing is more than spreadsheets, websites, databases, games and cyber; computing has fundamental roots in the nature of man's enquiry into reality. So how does all of this fit into our studies, and in particular the material presented in this and the following chapter? Perhaps a diagram may help.

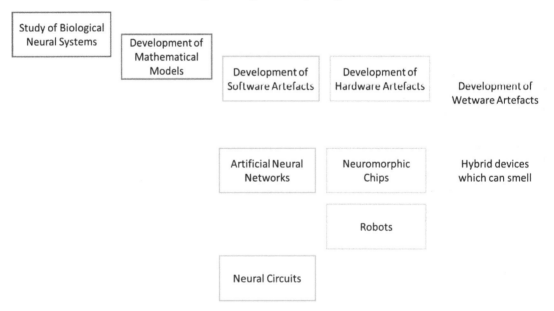

Reading from top left and moving across, the whole process of scientific discovery, modelling and simulation and finally application development is depicted. We start (top left) with a study of biological neural systems; this means observing sections of brain material, or *in vivo* experiments on animals or individual neural cells. Various Nobel Laureates such as Golgi and Cajal (1904) and Hubel and Weisel (1981) showed that neural systems are not just goo, they comprise individual elements called *neurons,* and these worked by processing electrical signals. This is truly fundamental; our brains work by electronics, and they have objects (neurons) which we can study!

Mathematical models of single neurons, and populations of neurons were developed by a huge number of research groups. These continue to be developed as new results come in from biological research. Mathematical models are important, since they can lead to the engineering of technological artefacts (software and hardware). These models can be crafted to simplify the complex nature of wet biology. Models can abstract out the annoying detail and give us a tractable (understandable) approach. Broadly speaking there are two flavours of models. The easiest one to understand sees the neuron as a 'leaky integrator' which responds to input values with a smoothly varying output response (Fig.8.1). The second model is perhaps closer to the biological and models the 'spikes' emitted by real neurons (Fig.8.2). This is currently the subject of active research.

Once the scientist and mathematicians have developed their mathematical models, the *engineers* can take over, and develop artefacts, and make money.

Let's think about *hardware* artefacts, known today as 'Neuromorphic Chips'. These are CPU chips which have a totally different architecture from the sequential, synchronously clocked processor or the parallel processing chips, both which separate processor from memory. Intel's Loihi-2 neuromorphic chip has 1 million neurons which can make 120 million connexions with other neurons, and of course these connexions can change strength, and finally it uses spiking neural architecture. There are a few applications of this technology.

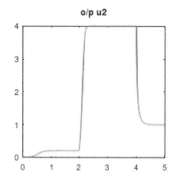

Figure 8.1 Leaky Integrator neuron. Response changes smoothly with time.

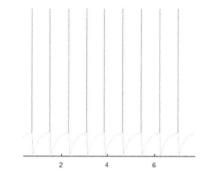

Figure 8.2 Spiking neuron model. Information is encoded as frequency of spikes.

Perhaps the most exciting development in this arena is the creating of new wetware artefacts. Here we have come full circle, and biological neurons are grown onto a silicon substrate to obtain some desired processing. Applications to odour detection have been made.

8.2 The Leaky Integrator Neuron

There are two important concepts you need to grasp. When a neuron receives an input, its internal state *changes*. Eventually this change stops, the state converges to an *equilibrium value* which is the final 'output' of the neuron. Let's take a physical example, a leaky water bucket.

Look at the diagram below where water is entering the bucket at a constant rate I and the leak is plugged.

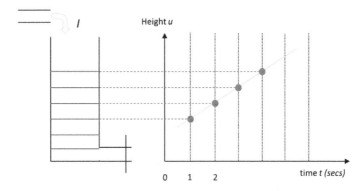

The height of the water is shown increasing with time. Since the water is coming in at a constant rate, then in each second the additional height is the same, so the height u rises on a straight line. We can write this mathematically like this, where the symbol Δu means change in height and the symbol Δu means change in time

$$\frac{\Delta u}{\Delta t} = I \qquad (1)$$

The left side of this expression is the rate of change of height due to the water coming in. The left side tells us 'the height of water is changing'. The right side I is the water flow. This tells us '*how* the water height is changing'. A larger I means that more water is coming in per second, so the rate of change of height (the left side) will be larger.

Now suppose the bucket is nearly full so we turn off the water supply, and open the tap (leak) at the bottom. Here's how the water level will change

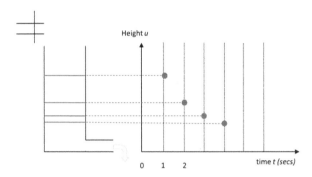

Of course, the water level falls, but not in a straight line. When the bucket is full, there is more water pushing down on the water in the pipe, so the flow through the pipe is larger. When the bucket is almost empty, there is little water pushing down on the water in the pipe, so the flow is reduced. A good model for the water rate of flow is proportional to the height, with a negative sign to show it's coming out,

$$-u$$

So the rate of change becomes

$$\frac{\Delta u}{\Delta t} = -u \qquad (2)$$

So, what happens when we have water coming in *and* leaking out at the same time. The *net* water coming in is just

$$I - u$$

so, the rate of change of water height is just

$$\frac{\Delta u}{\Delta t} = I - u \qquad (3)$$

A diagram may help. Imagine we let the water come in for a short time (with the leak closed) then stop the water coming in and open the leak and repeat this rather strange process. The water height might look something like this.

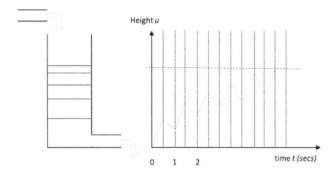

The amount of water that enters in each half-second is the same, so the rise in height is the same. But since the water height increases, the drop in height due to the leak gets larger and larger. So the height follows a curve which becomes flatter and flatter until is horizontal. You can see this from expression (3),

$$\frac{\Delta u}{\Delta t} = 0 \quad when \quad I = u$$

This is the *equilibrium* state of the bucket, the water height is proportional to the flow into the bucket[3].

There are a couple more points we must deal with before this model is complete. First, in the above discussion we have been thinking in discrete time steps Δt whereas in reality the height change is *continuous* with time. When we come to actually solving neural equations by software, we shall use continuous time. This needs a change in notation, so we replace Δt with a new symbol dt. Think of it like this, we make the change infinitesimally small,

$$\lim_{\Delta t \to 0} \Delta t = dt$$

so, our expression (3) becomes

---

[3] The astute reader will note that we have chosen not to introduce various constants in order to keep the maths clean.

$$\frac{du}{dt} = I - u$$

The second point concerns the size of the cross-sectional area of the bucket, glance over at Fig.8.3. If water flows in are the same for both buckets, then the one on the left will fill faster than the one on the right. It is more responsive; we say it has a smaller 'time constant' τ (pronounced 'tau'). This is incorporated into the expression like this,

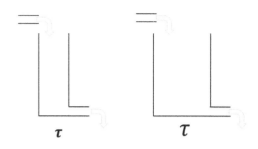

Figure 8.3 Buckets of different areas have different response times 'tau'

$$\frac{du}{dt} = \frac{1}{\tau}(-u + I) \qquad (4)$$

This is the final expression for the leaky bucket and is also the expression for all the leaky integrator neuros we shall use in this chapter. Let's summarise this as a graph.

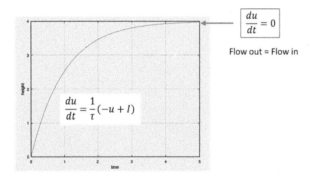

$$\frac{du}{dt} = 0$$

Flow out = Flow in

$$\frac{du}{dt} = \frac{1}{\tau}(-u + I)$$

Expression (4) is called a 'Ordinary Differential Equation' (ODE). We shall need one of these for each neuron in any circuit we construct. ODEs have application throughout science and engineering, and other disciplines such as business dynamics. Wherever something is changing, then and ODE solution springs to mind.

8.3 Some Basic Neural Circuits

Single Neuron with a Single Input

The neuron in Fig.8.4 has an input pulse of height I and it outputs its state u_1 which changes with time. We know how to model this neuron, it's just our leaky integrator,

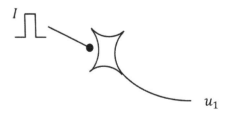

Figure 8.4 Single Neuron with a single input

$$\frac{du_1}{dt} = \frac{1}{\tau}(-u_1 + I) \qquad (5)$$

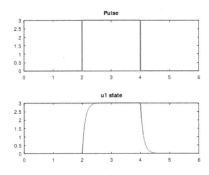

Figure 8.5 Single neuron response to input pulse of height 3

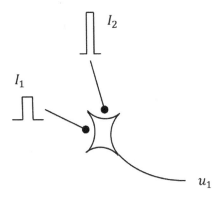

Figure 8.6 Neural circuit to add two variables

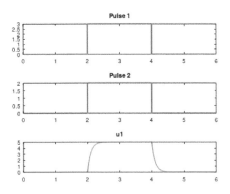

Figure 8.7 Adding two variables 3 and 2

with equilibrium solution

$$u_1(t \to \infty) = I$$

where we have made explicit that this happens as time approaches infinity. Fig.8.5 shows a typical solution for a pulse which rises to height $I=3$ then falls to zero. The neuron state steadily rises to 3, then falls gracefully to zero, in both cases it reaches the input value. You could think of this neural circuit as assigning a value to a variable.

Neural Addition

The circuit shown in Fig.8.6 is able to add two inputs. The black circle is called a *synapse* and is where an input comes into a neuron. The output tail from the neuron is called its *axon*.

We can write the expression for the neuron's behaviour as

$$\frac{du_1}{dt} = \frac{1}{\tau}(-u_1 + I_1 + I_2) \qquad (6)$$

since we have two inputs! The equilibrium solution is obtained by setting $\frac{du_1}{dt} = 0$ which gives us

$$-u_1 + I_1 + I_2$$

i.e.,

$$u_1 = I_1 + I_2$$

so we have added the inputs. This addition process for variables of values 3 and 2 is shown in Fig.8.7

Neural Subtraction

So far, we have assumed that the synapses (black) circles can be thought of making the neuron's state increase with time (like water coming in). These biological synapses are called *excitatory*. There are also synapses which behave in the opposite way, these *inhibitory* synapses have a negative effect on the neuron's state increase, just like sucking water out with a pump. These can be used to perform subtraction as shown in Fig.8.8.

Again, it's straightforward to write down the ODE for this circuit, we have

$$\frac{du_1}{dt} = \frac{1}{\tau}(-u_1 + I_1 - I_2) \qquad (7)$$

with equilibrium solution

$$u_1 = I_1 - I_2$$

Neural Multiplication

Recent research in biology has shown that individual neurons are able to carry out multiplication. The arrangement of the inputs is slightly different. One input makes synaptic contact with the neuron as usual, but the second input makes contact with the first, just before it reaches the neuron (Fig 8.9). This is called a *shunting* effect. In terms of water pipes, you can think of one pipe increasing or decreasing the flow of water in the main pipe.

The ODE is again quite straightforward

$$\frac{du_1}{dt} = \frac{1}{\tau}(-u_1 + I_1 I_2) \qquad (8)$$

with equilibrium solution

$$u_1 = I_1 I_2$$

8.4 Applications to Autonomous Robots

Robot with steering

Here we have an autonomous robot which is driven by two rear wheels which rotate with the same speed and turns by rotating the front driving wheel. The object is to build a neural circuit so the robot will turn towards the light. Taking inspiration from biological critters, we use two sensor neurons and two motor neurons. The problem is how to wire these up to obtain the desired behaviour (Fig.8.10).

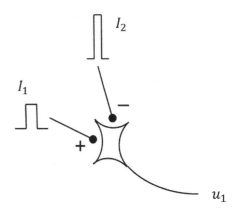

Figure 8.8 Neural Subtraction using inhibition on input-2

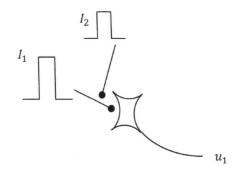

Figure 8.9 Neural multiplication using 'shunting'

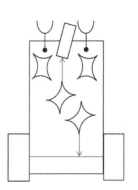

Figure 8.10 Robot with steering showing 2 sensory neurons and 2 motor neurons

It's easy to understand that the sensor (eye) nearest to the light will receive more light and therefore provide greater input to its associated neuron. Also, if the light is in front at the centre, then both these neurons will receive the same excitation, any difference in their outputs will indicate the light is to one side and the front wheel should turn. So, we need to calculate the difference and use this to drive the front motor like this.

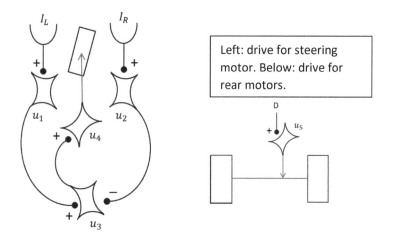

For the input sensory neurons, we have

$$\frac{du_1}{dt} = \frac{1}{\tau}(-u_1 + I_L)$$

$$\frac{du_2}{dt} = \frac{1}{\tau}(-u_2 + I_R)$$

then find the difference

$$\frac{du_3}{dt} = \frac{1}{\tau}(-u_3 + u_1 - u_2)$$

then drive the steering motor neuron

$$\frac{du_4}{dt} = \frac{1}{\tau}(-u_4 + u_3)$$

and drive the rear wheel neuron

$$\frac{du_5}{dt} = \frac{1}{\tau}(-u_5 + D)$$

where D is a constant value to produce a steady forward speed. This circuit is probably over-complex you could build a solution with just two neurons in total, but if nature had to solve this problem, then that's a probable solution. Working down these ODEs solving each for its equilibrium state we find

$$u_1 = I_L \qquad u_2 = I_R$$

$$u_3 = u_1 - u_2 \quad = I_L - I_R$$

$$u_4 = u_3 = I_L - I_R$$

so, the motor drive u_4 is the difference between the sensor inputs and can be positive and negative. Finally, we must make the wheel turn in the correct direction. The solution of the motor driving the rear wheels is simply $u_5 = D$.

Braitenberg Vehicles

These are differential-drive robots introduced by Valentino Braitenberg as experiments in 'Synthetic Psychology'. Again we have two sensory and two motor neurons, and movement towards the light is achieved by cross-coupling left and right sensory and motor neurons, with exciting synapses, Fig. 8.11. The ODEs are straightforward

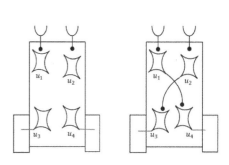

Figure 8.11 Braitenberg Vehicle Problem (left) and Solution (right).

$$\frac{du_1}{dt} = \frac{1}{\tau}(-u_1 + I_L)$$

$$\frac{du_2}{dt} = \frac{1}{\tau}(-u_2 + I_R)$$

and for the motor neurons

$$\frac{du_3}{dt} = \frac{1}{\tau}(-u_3 + u_2)$$

$$\frac{du_4}{dt} = \frac{1}{\tau}(-u_4 + u_1)$$

with equilibrium solutions $u_3 = I_R$ and $u_4 = I_L$ which drive the wheels to make the robot turn correctly

8.5 A Jump Aside – Some Puzzles

Work out what these circuits do: output(s) in terms of input(s). Solutions from the author

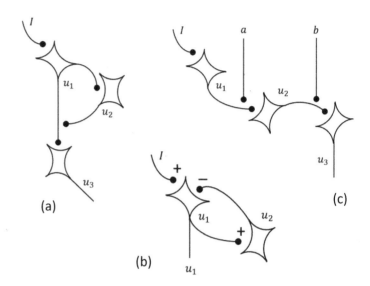

(a)

(b)

(c)

8.6 Enhancing the Leaky Integrator Model

So far, the neuron has successfully performed some *linear* operations such as summing the input signals. But there is a better model of a neuron which has an additional processing stage following the summation. So, we can think of our enhanced neuron as having two parts. Fig.8.12 and we express this like this; the output of the *i*'th neuron is

$$o_i = f(u_i)$$

where the u_i is the internal state of the *i*'th neuron, just what we have been working with so far. This may not make too much sense (because it's abstract). So, let's look at a concrete example of an output function

Threshold Output Function

Here the output function takes the neuron state u_i and if it is above some threshold value θ which you can choose, then the

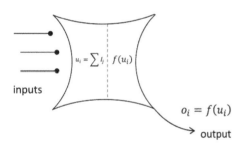

Figure 8.12 Enhanced neuron model with output function

neuron output is 1, else it is zero. This function is shown in Fig.8.13. To understand this, let's take a worked example

Let's assume that all the neuron levels are in the range between 0 and 1. So what do the following two circuits output when the threshold is set to 0.5?

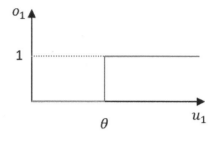

Figure 8.13 Threshold output function.

Well in both cases the value of the neurons state is 1+0=1 and this is above the threshold value of 0.5, so we get an output of 1. Now think about the following two cases

In the first case the neuron state is 0+0=0 which is below the threshold, so the output is 0. In the second case the neuron state is 1+1=2 which is greater than the threshold, so the output is 1. Putting all this into a table we find

input 1	input 2	state	output
0	0	0	0
0	1	1	1
1	0	1	1
1	0	2	1

So, this neuron functions as an OR-gate.

The NAND-Gate

All computer electronics (CPU and memory) can be built from a load of NAND-gates. If we can find a neural circuit for a NAND gate, then we can build an entire computer out of neurons. It's quite easy really.

First, we create a neural AND gate. A bit of thought shows all we need is a two-input neuron with a threshold set to say 1.5 so that only an input (1,1) will raise the neuron's state above the threshold and output a 1. That's an AND gate. To get a NAND, we need to follow our AND by a NOT gate, so we must design a neural NOT gate or 'invertor'. Consider the single input neural circuit shown in Fig.8.14. If we design the neuron so its state follows this ODE

$$\frac{du_1}{dt} = \frac{1}{\tau}(-u_1 - I + 1)$$

then we find its equilibrium state is

$$u_1 = 1 - I$$

so, if the input is 0 the output is 1 and if the input is 1 the output is zero. The threshold function will guarantee a nice clean output of exactly 1 or 0, the inverse of the input. We have a NOT gate. Therefore, we have a NAND gate.

Since we have a NAND gate, we have proved that all electronic circuits can be built from neurons.

8.7 Shunting feedback – A new type of neuron

Here we are going to invent a new type of *nonlinear* neuron. It demonstrates the power we have at creating new systems, but I must admit, there *is* biological support for our invention. We will *not* be using an output function in this case; the inherent nonlinearity will do this job for us.

The idea is shown in the diagram below. On the left we start with our simple linear neuron which has a constant input of 1.0, the usual ODE is shown. Now we take a leap of faith, and we multiply the output of this neuron, u_1 by itself, using the concept of shunting which we have seen earlier. This gives us a new ODE which has interesting solutions.

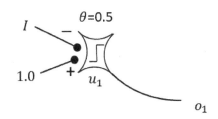

Figure 8.14 Neural NOT gate

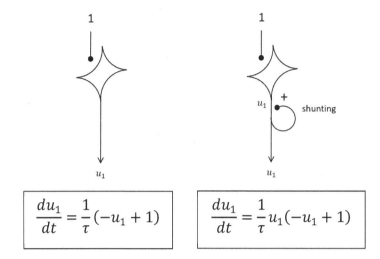

$$\frac{du_1}{dt} = \frac{1}{\tau}(-u_1 + 1)$$

$$\frac{du_1}{dt} = \frac{1}{\tau}u_1(-u_1 + 1)$$

You can see the inclusion of shunting; the bracket for the neuron on the left is multiplied by the value of the neuron's state u_1. The equilibrium solutions for our new neuron on the right are simply the solutions of this expression

$$u_1(-u_1 + 1) = 0$$

and there are two: $u_1 = 0$ and $u_1 = 1$. Logic levels again. But we are not complete since we must test the *stability* of these two solutions. That means setting u_1 to a small value close to 0, and looking whether the circuit solution returns to 0, or diverges from it.

For $u_1 = 0.1$ we find that $du_1/dt = 0.09$, so the solution grows away from $u_1 = 0$. Unstable. Also, for $u_1 = -0.1$ we find that $du_1/dt = -0.11$, so again the solution diverges from 0 (it becomes even more negative). So, the solution 0 is *unstable* and the circuit will not converge to this solution.

Now for the other fixed point 1.0, we try dropping down to $u_1 = 0.9$ and here we find $du_1/dt = 0.09$ so the solution rises up back to 1.0, looking good. For $u_1 = 1.1$, just above 1.0 we find that $du_1/dt = -0.11$ so the solution returns back down to 1.0. Hence the solution 1.0 is *stable* and we expect the circuit to display this value at equilibrium.

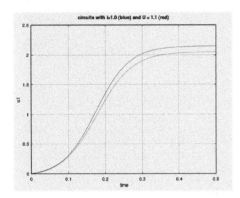

Figure 8.15 Response of the shunting circuit to two inputs: 1.0 (blue) and 1,1 (red)

Now let's develop this shunting circuit a little. First, we need to add an input. The ODE now looks like this

$$\frac{du_1}{dt} = \frac{1}{\tau}u_1(-u_1 + 1 + I_1)$$

Let's see how this circuit responds to two different inputs, starting from a neural state u_1 close to zero. The results for two inputs, 1.0 and 1.1 are shown in Fig. 8.15. The results are unsurprising but important, the curve corresponding to the larger input always lies above the other curve and reaches a higher equilibrium value. This tells us that *the rate of increase* of the neural state is larger when the input is larger.

8.8 Application – Finding an array maximum

Here we shall use the above shunting circuit and develop an exciting application, a neural circuit which can find and output the maximum number in an array of numbers. The time taken to do this does not increase with the length of the array. This is an incredible result and cannot be achieved using procedural code.

Consider the circuit below with $I_1 = 4.5$ and $I_2 = 5.5$. The dynamics of the circuit is also shown

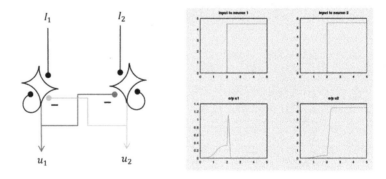

First the circuit; we have taken two of our shunting neurons and have coupled them together, through the colored lines. Note that the coupling is *inhibitory* and as we shall see soon it is *shunting inhibition*. We start with the input values, so what happens next? Both the values of u_1 and u_2 will increase, but u_2 will rise faster than u_1. Since u_2 is larger its shunting inhibition (green line) on u_1 will be larger than the reciprocal inhibition of u_1 on u_2 (red line). So u_2 (which was already rising faster) will rise even faster. This process continues until u_2 effectively kills (quenches) u_1. The circuit has selected the larger input!

Now let's have a look at the ODEs. To help out, a 'key' is provided in Fig.8.16 reminding us of the origin of each term. We have two 'symmetric' equations

$$\frac{du_1}{dt} = \frac{1}{\tau} u_1(-u_1 + 1 - ku_2 + I_1)$$

$$\frac{du_2}{dt} = \frac{1}{\tau} u_2(-u_2 + 1 - ku_1 + I_2)$$

If we assume that both neurons have identical initial values, $u_1(t = 0) = u_1(t = 0) = \epsilon$ where ϵ is a small number, then the only difference between them is the value of the neurons' inputs. This will establish their initial growth rates which, as discussed above will be different. The term ku_2, inhibition from neuron-2 into neuron 1 will be larger than the reciprocal term ku_1, inhibition from neuron-1 into neuron-2 if $u_2 > u_1$ which will be the case if $I_2 > I_1$, so neuron-1's growth will slow down faster than neuron-2's growth.

Eventually neuron-1 will be killed to zero, so the expression for neuron-2 will become

$$\frac{du_2}{dt} = \frac{1}{\tau} u_2(-u_2 + 1 + I_2)$$

and the equilibrium solution of this is simply

$$u_2 = 1 + I_2$$

in other words, neuron-2 converges to a value equal to its input plus 1. So, these two neurons form a 'winner takes all' circuit, which provides us with the largest input value (plus one).

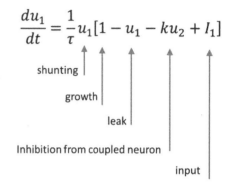

$$\frac{du_1}{dt} = \frac{1}{\tau} u_1[1 - u_1 - ku_2 + I_1]$$

shunting

growth

leak

Inhibition from coupled neuron

input

Figure 8.16 Meaning of individual terms

It's easy to generalize this to an array of N-elements. The circuit shown below for an array of 3 elements has one additional neuron to give us the maximum value in the array. It adds the outputs from the shunting inhibition layer (only one will be non-zero) and subtracts 1 to give us the maximum value in the input array.

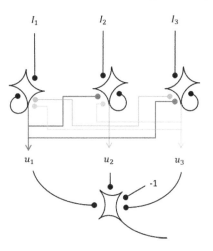

The shunting layer will send the largest input value (plus 1) to the final neuron which subtracts 1 and outputs the maximum value. The diagram below shows the parallel neural processing for input values (2.4, 1.3, 3.2), the largest value 3.2 has been correctly output.

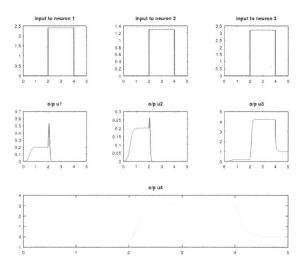

Sure there are some 'pathologies', e.g., if all inputs are the same value, then all outputs u_i are the same and are summed. It's fairly straightforward to show that for N neurons, the final output is

$$\left(\frac{I+1}{1+(N-1)k}\right)N-1$$

This is left as an exercise for the interested reader.

8.9 Procedural Programming with Neural Circuits

We have seen that computer hardware can be replaced with neural circuits, so we can build a computer out of *wetware*. Now comes my conjecture that procedural programming can be replaced by neural circuits. This means we have to show how these circuits can replace the three basic programming constructs: *sequence, selection* and *iteration.* Currently I have two out of the three, perhaps you can supply the missing link.

A Neural Selection Circuit

Here we shall see how to create the if-then-else construct. Take a simple example

```
if(input > threshold) {
    x = 6.0;
} else {
    x = 2.0;
}
```

There are two different things going on here. First, we have the *logic* of selection or 'control flow' where the if statement has a condition whose outcome is *binary,* we either select the if-block or the else block. Then within each block we have a variable assignment. This is 'data flow'. We construct a neural circuit keeping these two dimensions of processing separate. Take the control flow. This is shown in the diagram below.

The input arrives at the first neuron which has a threshold set at `threshold`. So, the first neuron will output 1.0 when the input is above the threshold, in other words it has generated the 'if' control signal, activating the 'if' block of code.

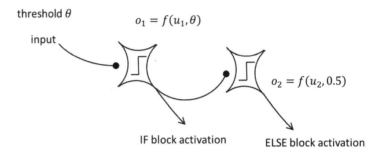

The equation for the first neuron state is simple

$$\frac{du_1}{dt} = \frac{1}{\tau}(-u_1 + input)$$

and the equation for the second neuron state is just our inverter

$$\frac{du_2}{dt} = \frac{1}{\tau}(-u_2 - o_1 + 1)$$

To complete the circuit, we need a third neuron to represent the value of the x-variable which is quite straightforward (Fig. 8.17).

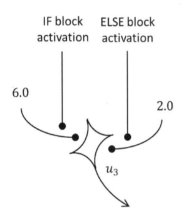

Figure 8.17 Assigning values to a variable based on if(condition)

Sequences of procedural statements

As neural circuit engineers we have considerable freedom in designing circuit which will produce sequences of pulses, based of course on biological neurons. Biology reveals to us several mechanisms of sequence generation; there are *neural oscillators* (which we shall meet in the next chapter), *spiking neurons* (which may be addressed in the future. But here we shall consider *chains of neuron delays*. Before we get into the details, let's have a look at the *concept* we are proposing, shown in the diagram below.

Let's consider a sequence of two maths operations; first we add two variables (A + B) and when sufficient time has passed for this to complete, we multiply the result by a third variable C, so we end up with C x (A + B).

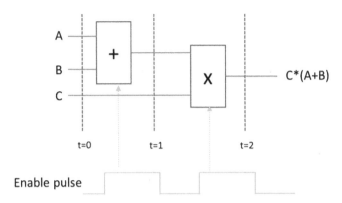

The two blue rectangles show processing blocks, an adder and a multiplier; we know how to do these using neural circuits, so imagine the circuits are inside the blocks. Now we know that neural processing takes time (remember 'tau') so the multiplication must be delayed until the addition is complete. That is the crux of the concept. The green enable pulse first enables ('switches on') the adder, and when addition is complete, it switches the adder off. Then, a little later it switches the multiplier on which does the second operation. So, we have a sequence.

The only question remaining is how to we produce the green pulse train? This is quite straightforward, we need a chain of threshold neurons, each will provide a delay and output a pulse like this

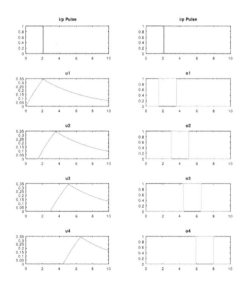

Figure 8.18 Pulse Sequence Generator: Red input to neural chain; blue neuron states; green thresholded outputs.

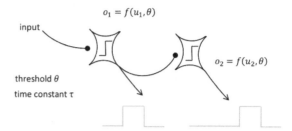

An example of the behaviour of a short chain is shown in Fig.8.18 showing a clear series of pulses.

The whole process depends on choosing a correct time constant *and* a corresponding threshold. If we specify the threshold value τ and the length of the pulse; we want T then it turns out the required threshold is

$$\theta = 1 - \frac{1}{2 - e^{-\frac{T}{\tau}}}$$

as shown in the appendix. The results shown in Fig.8.18 were produced for a pulse length of 2 secs and a time constant f 5 secs, with a computed threshold 0.255372.

8.10 Numerical Solution of ODEs

Often when we get a solution to a mathematical equation, it is a single number like 33.01. Solutions to ordinary differential equations ODEs are not single numbers, they tell you how something is changing with time, like the predicted GDP of a country. We have seen this in our work where neuron states change with time.

So how do we solve our ODEs? Since they change with time, we must have a starting time and a starting value for each component of our system; these are called the *initial conditions* for our system. For the water bucket model, the initial conditions were {time = 0, height = 0}. Then we proceed to *advance the solution over time,* and we do this using the associated ODE which after all, tells us how something changes with time!

Here's one simple approach. Let's revisit the leaky bucket where the rate of change in height was

$$\frac{du}{dt} = \frac{1}{\tau}(-u + I)$$

So we could consider a time interval Δt and calculate the change in height during that interval

$$\Delta u = \frac{du}{dt}\Delta t$$

and inserting the expression for du/dt we have

$$\Delta u = \frac{1}{\tau}(-u + I)\Delta t$$

Say we have $\tau = 1$ and $I = 2$ and the bucket starts empty so that $u(t = 0) = 0$. Choosing a time step $\Delta t = 0.1$, then in this interval the change in height is

$$\Delta u = \frac{1}{1.0}(-0.0 + 2.0)0.1 \quad = \quad 0.2$$

so the value of u is now 0.2. We then take another time step and repeat the calculation

$$\Delta u = \frac{1}{1.0}(-0.2 + 2.0)0.1 \quad = \quad 0.18$$

so the value of u is now $0.2 + 0.18 = 0.38$. And so we continue advancing the solution. If we were casting this into code, we could write something like this

```
dT = 0.1;
time = 0;
u = 0;
while(time < tEnd) {
    dudt = (-u + In)/tau;
    u = u + du;
    time = time + dT;
}
```

This simple approach may work (for simple systems) and is known as the Euler (pronounced oiler) approach. The issue is how to we choose the time interval Δt? It turns out that the accuracy of the computed solution depends on this time interval, more accuracy means a smaller time interval, but this means more computations. You see the problem.

Fortunately, numerical solvers have been developed where you can specify the desired accuracy, and the solver will adapt the time step to give you your desired accuracy, and it can change the time step on the fly! One such solver in the Runge-Kutta-Fehlberg 'ode45' solver which we shall use for most of our ODE problems.

We need two files. First the 'main' file where we set up parameters, set initial conditions, do our plotting and of course make a call to the **ode45** solver. Here's some lines from the main Octave script where the solver is called, and the result extracted and plotted. See provided files for more detail.

```
[t,u] = ode45(@rhs_SinglePulse,[tstart,tend],uinit,options);
u1 = u(:,1);
plot(t,u1);
```

Note the call @rhs_SinglePulse. This is the 'right hand side' of the ODE and is found in the file with the same name. Here's a typical rhs file

```
1   function
dudt=rhs_SinglePulse(t,u)
2   global tau In
3   dudt = zeros(1,1);
4   dudt(1) = ( -u(1) + In)/tau;
5   endfunction
```

The function outputs dudt (from the maths du/dt) as you can see in line 1. Line 2 allows us to access global variables set in the main script. Line 3 created the variable dudt which is always an array (here length = 1) then line 4 does the computation.

This function is passed to the `ode45(` … `)` function as a parameter. The latter function makes repeated calls to the 'rhs' until the final time `tend` is reached.

Chapter 9
Neural Oscillators

9.1 A brief Introduction

Neural oscillators are all around us, in fact some of the most important ones are *inside* us, I am thinking of the neural oscillators which make our heat beat, our lungs breathe, our gut transport food down the digestive tract, and of course the neural circuits which drive the motor neurons in our legs to make us walk. Neural oscillation also features in many disorders such as synchronization of brain neurons during epileptic seizures, tremors in Parkinson's disease patients, and disruption of cortical oscillation in schizophrenia.

All of the above are of great interest within computing, where computational solutions of the underlying mathematical models will further our understanding. But perhaps the most interesting application of modelling neural oscillators is in robotics, in particular those circuits which enable legged robots to walk, segmented robots to swim and crawl. This application area is called 'Central Pattern Generators' (CPGs). The idea is that a small neural circuit will drive tetrapod/quadruped legs (think a horse) to make it move with a number of different *gaits* (canter, trot, gallop). In this chapter we shall work up to an understanding of hexapod (beetle) gaits.

9.2 Oscillation Refresher

Before we get into the details, let's just review our understanding of simple *mechanical* oscillations with which we are all familiar. Let's take a car suspension as an example, Fig.9.1 shows a Land Rover spring and a simple model, the Land Rover body mass (yellow) on the spring, the bottom of which is resting on the ground (we've neglected the wheel and tyre in the model). This is a simple *mass-spring* system.

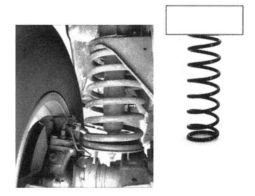

Figure 9.1 Land Rover Suspension and model.

When you are driving along and hit a bump, then the spring gets compressed, and the car body will oscillate up and down as shown in the diagram below. The body starts at **a** and as time progresses, passes through **b, c, d,** and back to **a** where the cycle of oscillation starts again. Note the red arrows show how the body is moving at these snapshots in time.

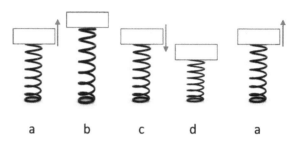

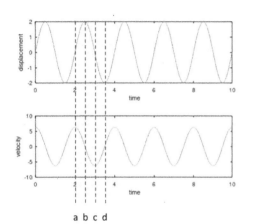

Figure 9.2 Displacement and Velocity of an oscillating Land Rover

When we model the suspension (mathematically) and plot out the solution, then we find the *displacement* and *velocity* of the car body change as shown in Fig.9.2. These have been labelled according to the above diagram. What do these tell us? This is not easy to answer, since we must look at two plots and the diagram, a bit like playing the organ[4].

Well at **a** there is no displacement, but the Land Rover body has positive velocity which means it moves upwards until it reaches its maximum displacement at **b.** Here its velocity is zero. Then the body velocity becomes negative, it is moving down. So, its displacement decreases, and it passes through zero displacement **c** where the velocity is its largest (negative) value. Then it slows down, and at **d** it has stopped (zero velocity) with the largest negative displacement. Then its velocity becomes positive, so it rises again until it hits its starting state **a**. One cycle of oscillation is complete, the rest is repetition!

Looking at Fig.9.2 we see something interesting. Both displacement and velocity are oscillating with the same period, around 2 sec. The peak of the velocity seems to 'follow' the peak of the displacement. So, displacement and

---

[4] I am learning the organ at the moment, so you have my symphony.

velocity are both *periodic in time*. They are clearly related, so this raises the question how could we show this relationship? The answer is fundamentally important to understand oscillating systems, this is the *concept* of the **phase plane**.

The diagram below reproduces Fig.9.2 with the addition of the *phase plane* on the right, a plot of displacement versus velocity.

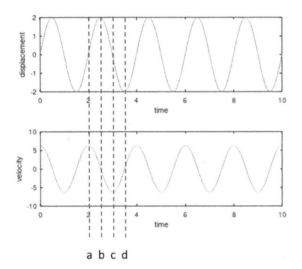
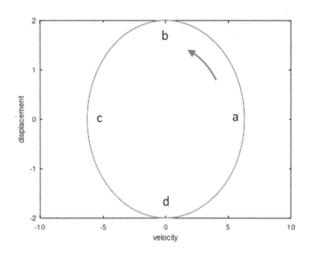

This result is quite amazing; we get a closed curve! We start at **a** then progress through **b, c, d** and back to **a**. Then we go around the curve again (the red arrow shows the direction of motion around this curve). This works because both displacement and velocity are periodic, with the same period.

This *trajectory* of our suspension system in the *phase plane* is quite fundamental, and in general tells us a lot about an oscillating system. The phase plane combines displacement and velocity, but we have lost an explicit representation of time. Of course, we can recover this by using a coded solution.

So, let's develop this further for our Land Rover Suspension system. When the Land Rover hits a bump, it starts to oscillate, but the oscillations are damped (removed) by the suspension shock absorbers. Let's see how the above diagrams change.

The blue plots reproduce the above, the red plots show the effect of damping. Both the Land Rover body displacement and velocity decay down to zero; it stops moving (zero velocity) and approaches its 'sleeping' location (zero).

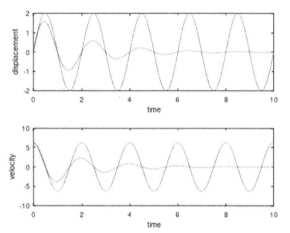

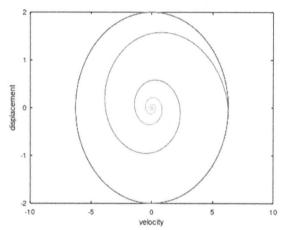

All this information is contained in the phase plot. The red spiral trajectory, moving inwards (0,0) clearly shows that both the Land Rover suspension displacement and body velocity decrease with time and end up at zero.

Now let's do something hypothetical and see what happens if we add energy into the suspension system rather than taking it away. A simple computation yields the following result.

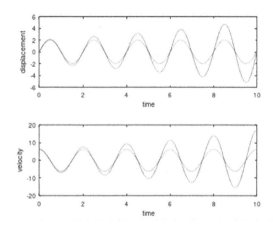

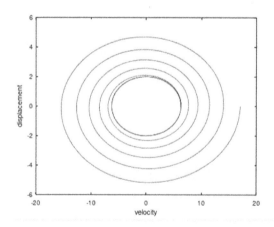

Both displacement and velocity increase with time due to the added energy, the trajectory on the phase plane is a spiral expanding outwards. This is quite an unstable system and would spell disaster for a physical suspension system.

In summary, we see three sorts of trajectories on the phase plane. First is the stable closed ellipse. In general, this can be any smooth shape, and is called a **limit cycle**. The other trajectories either move towards this limit cycle or move away from it.

9.3 Building an Oscillator from Leaky Integrators

Here we shall attempt to build a neural oscillator by connecting two leaky integrator neurons together. We shall discover that it is possible to create an oscillator, but also that this is useless, and cannot exist in a real biological system.

The first thing to note is that a single leaky integrator neuron cannot oscillate; we have investigated single neurons in detail, and we have never experienced oscillation. So, we turn to two neurons and think how to make these oscillate. If we put them in a chain, one after the other then again, we will not get oscillations. The only possibility is if we connect the output of the second to the input of the first, so we have a feedback loop, rather like a microphone close to a loudspeaker which produces a howl.

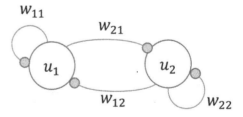

Figure 9.3 Two neurons totally connected with each other

Let's take two neurons and consider the general case where each neuron is connected to each other neuron, including itself. This is shown in Fig.9.3. The strengths of the connexions between the neurons are shown as the 'w' symbols, where w_{ij} is the strength of connexion from neuron j into neuron i. So w_{12} concerns the output of neuron-2 coming into the input of neuron-1, and w_{11} shows the input of neuron-1 from its own output.

Now let's write down some possible equations for two leaky integrators connected. This is straightforward and follows from the material presented in Chapter 5.

$$\frac{du_1}{dt} = \frac{1}{\tau}(-u_1 + w_{12}u_2)$$

$$\frac{du_2}{dt} = \frac{1}{\tau}(-u_2 + w_{21}u_1)$$

The first terms on the right in both equations are the integrator leak, and the second terms are the coupling from the other neuron. So, we view the leak as a neuron coupled to itself. We can write the above equations in matrix form

$$\begin{bmatrix} \dot{u}_1 \\ \dot{u}_2 \end{bmatrix} = \begin{bmatrix} -1 & w_{12} \\ w_{21} & -1 \end{bmatrix} \begin{bmatrix} u_1 \\ u_2 \end{bmatrix}$$

Now, the theory of linear systems (see appendix) tells us that if this system will oscillate then the *trace* of the matrix must be zero, Here the trace is -1 + -1 which is -2 which is not zero. So, we must add a positive coupling from at least one neuron into itself, let's call this *a* and do this for neuron-1. Then we have

$$\begin{bmatrix} \dot{u}_1 \\ \dot{u}_2 \end{bmatrix} = \begin{bmatrix} a-1 & w_{12} \\ w_{21} & -1 \end{bmatrix} \begin{bmatrix} u_1 \\ u_2 \end{bmatrix}$$

Now the trace is $(a-2)$ and since this has to be zero, we find that $a = 2$. No other value will do. This turns out to be a real problem, but we shall come back to this, since there is another condition on the above system if it is to oscillate. The *determinant* of the matrix must be greater than zero. For the above matrix this means

$$(a-1)(-1) - w_{12}w_{21} > 0$$

which simplifies to

$$w_{12}w_{21} < -1$$

This result tells us that one of the interconnections must be excitatory and one inhibitory, so the product is a negative

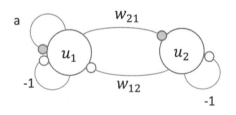

Figure 9.4 Leaky integrator oscillator circuit

number (and less than -1). So, our leaky integrator oscillator circuit looks like Fig.9.4 where excitatory and inhibitory synapses have been clearly indicated.

While this neural circuit will work, it will only work in theory. The problem is that the value of *a* needs to be fixed to an *exact* value, *a* = 2. Mathematically this is possible, but it is infeasible in a biological system which functions using chemicals whose concentrations may have a range of values. Your heart does not stop beating when you have a cup of coffee (which affects levels of methylxanthine in your system). A similar conclusion could be reached thinking about solving the above system on a digital computer; you set the value of *a* like this `a = 2.0;` but the CPU represents this number with a finite number of bits, and there is no guarantee that its representation is exactly 2.0. Glance at Fig.9.5 which shows my computer's solution which is not a steady oscillation. The behaviour is hardware dependent, it is not robust to changes unlike a biological system. My heart beats, so does yours and at about the same rate.

There is another *nasty* property of the leaky-integrator oscillator, which is also shared by the Land Rover suspension. This concerns the *amplitude* of the oscillation. The above theory does not predict a value for the amplitude, so we conclude this could be anything from 0.1 to a million. The trajectory in phase space could be of any size. Biology does not like such unknowns; all our hearts beat with approximately the same amplitude.

9.4 Biological Neural Oscillators

Recordings of neural oscillators *in vivo* have been made at a number of scales from small collections of neurons to larger interacting populations, especially in the brain cortex. These have been successfully modelled such as the FitzHugh – Nagumo model of small collections, or the Wilson-Cowan equations for the cortex. Studies reveal that real neurons emit periodic pulses or bursts of oscillations. These are called 'spiking' neurons, see Fig.9.6. Computational models of

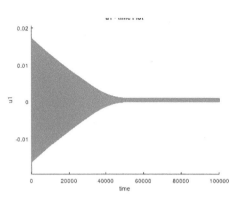

Figure 9.5 Solution of leaky integrator oscillator where the value of a has been set to 2.0 in the code.

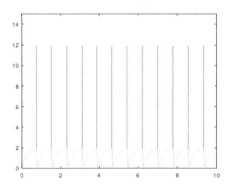

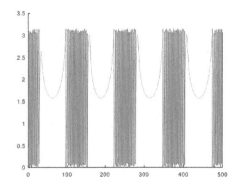

Figure 9.6 Simulation of 'spiking' neurons. Top Integrate and Fire, bottom Atoll models

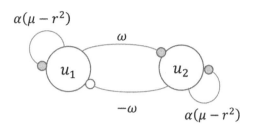

Figure 9.7 Structure of the Hopf neural oscillator

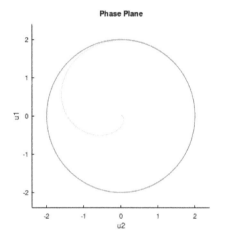

Figure 9.8 Limit Cycle for the Hopf oscillator

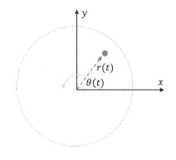

Figure 9.9 Polar coordinate description of the phase plane

spiking neurons are used mainly to understand biological neurons rather than applications in engineering scenarios such as Central Pattern Generators for legged or segmented robot motion. We shall study the simplest model which captures the fundamental behaviour of most neural oscillators, the Hopf oscillator (Fig 9.7). Later we shall apply this to the locomotion of a hexapod robot.

9.5 The Hopf Oscillator

This comprises a pair of neurons, and its structure is very similar to the leaky-integrator model discussed (and rejected) above. Each neuron influences itself and is connected to the other neuron. Like the leaky-integrator oscillator, one of these inter-connections is excitatory and the other is inhibitory. Here are the equations for the neurons

$$\frac{du_1}{dt} = \alpha(\mu - r^2)u_1 - \omega u_2$$

$$\frac{du_2}{dt} = \omega u_1 + \alpha(\mu - r^2)u_2$$

where there are three parameters, α, μ and ω and the variable r is just

$$r = \sqrt{u_1^2 + u_2^2}$$

Looking at the two ODEs, the feedback term in each neuron depends on $(\mu - r^2)$ so if r is small then this is positive, and the values of both neurons will grow. But if $r^2 > \mu$ then the feedback is negative, and the values of both neurons will fall. In fact, the trajectory in the phase plane moves to a circle of radius $\sqrt{\mu}$. This is a stable *limit cycle* which attracts all trajectories in the phase plane, Fig.9.8. The above ODEs for the neurons can be transformed to polar coordinates (radius r angle θ) as shown in Fig.9.9.

$$\frac{dr}{dt} = \alpha(\mu - r^2)r$$

$$\frac{d\theta}{dt} = \omega$$

The first expression shows how the radius of the trajectory point changes with time, and the second expression shows how the angle changes with time. You can see that the angle changes at a constant rate ω which defines the frequency of the oscillator. The right-hand-side of the first expression is positive if $r^2 < \mu$ causing r to increase, and it's negative if $r^2 > \mu$ which causes r to decrease. When $r^2 = \mu$ then the right-hand-side is zero, so r does not change. This shows that the trajectory will always approach the limit cycle, which for the Hopf oscillator is a circle.

9.6 Phase Lag Neurons

When we come to modelling insect gaits, we shall find that their legs oscillate with the same frequency, but there is a phase lag between legs, e.g., a 180 degree phase lag means one leg is moving forwards (raised off the ground) and the next one is moving backwards (on the ground) so the bug moves forwards.

This can be achieved with a single leaky-integrator neuron

$$\frac{du}{dt} = \frac{1}{\tau}(-u + I)$$

where the input is e.g., $I = \sin \omega t$ which is a sine wave with frequency ω. The output u of the neuron is another sine wave with amplitude

$$\frac{I}{\sqrt{1 + \tau^2 \omega^2}}$$

which is always less than I and with a phase lag given by

$$\tan \varphi = \omega \tau$$

Now we use these results to *engineer* a neuron which provides us with a desired phase lag but keeps the amplitude constant. Since the frequency of the sine wave is given (e.g.,

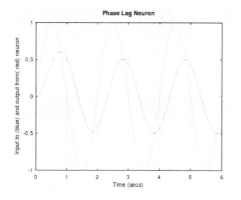

Figure 9.10 Input (blue) and output (red) from a single neuron giving a phase difference of 60 degrees

by the Hopf oscillator) then we use the time constant τ to set our desired phase,

$$\tau = \frac{\tan \varphi}{\omega}$$

Now to restore the amplitude to its original value I we must multiply the input to the neuron by the factor by which the amplitude was decreased, namely $\sqrt{1 + \tau^2 \omega^2}$. So, our engineered neuron becomes

$$\frac{du}{dt} = \frac{1}{\tau}(-u + kI)$$

where

$$k = \sqrt{1 + \tau^2 \omega^2}.$$

This neural circuit works well, it was used to create the phase lag shown in Fig.9.10.

There is one complication; due to the nature of the tangent function, this circuit can produce a maximum phase shift of 90 degrees, and often we need more than that. The solution is to use a chain of, say 3 neurons, and get each to provide 1/3 of the total lag we need. The neural circuit sketched below shows just such a chain with the sine wave produced by our friend, the Hopf oscillator.

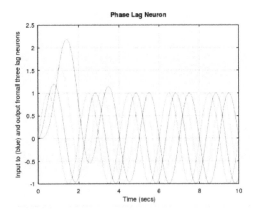

Figure 9.11 Phases along chain of three neurons, the total phase lag is 180 degrees

Fig.9.11 shows the output of such a chain which was asked to produce a total phase shift of 180 degrees. You can see this by comparing the light blue curve (input) and the purple curve (output). The only slight issue is that it takes a certain time for the chain to settle, there is a clear initial transient which lasts around 4 seconds or so.

9.7 Insect Gait Patterns – The Hexapod

Previous Work

Biological systems (creatures) have provided much inspiration for generations of engineered robots that can walk, crawl or swim. One of the most influential observations for segmented creatures such as fish was the propagation of a wave of oscillation down the length of the creature. If the creature were cut into two, then each part would continue to show this wave. These observations led to the idea that the neural circuit consisted of a *coupled chain of oscillators* rather than just one master oscillator.

Most previous work has adopted this architecture, e.g., the hexapod shown below comprises six oscillators (neuron pairs) one for each leg.

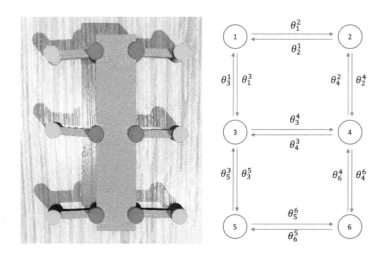

The neural circuit for this model is quite complex, the equation for each neural oscillator has the form

$$\begin{bmatrix} \dot{x}_i \\ \dot{z}_i \end{bmatrix} = \begin{bmatrix} \alpha(\mu - r_i^2) & -\omega \\ \omega & \alpha(\mu - r_i^2) \end{bmatrix} \begin{bmatrix} x_i \\ z_i \end{bmatrix} + \sum_{j \neq i} R(\theta_j^i) \begin{bmatrix} 0 \\ x_j + z_j \\ r_j \end{bmatrix}$$

where the rightmost term captures the coupling into the i'th oscillator from the other oscillators connected to it. You will recognize the Hopf oscillator here. See appendix for maths.

Our Approach

We do not need a chain of coupled oscillators since we shall agree not to cut up our robot into bits. Our approach is to use a single Hopf oscillator, then circuits of phase shift neurons to drive the legs and feet in the correct sequence.

So, let's see what we need to achieve. The literature reports the various gaits in a number of ways. For our hexapod there are three principal gaits: metachronal (wave), tetrapod (ripple), and tripod. One way of reporting these gaits is the phase lag of each leg. I use the left front leg as the reference (absolute phase is 0).

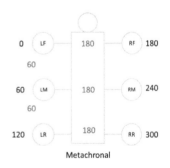

Metachronal

Ripple   Tripod

Perhaps the easiest to understand is the tripod gait; the legs move in three triplets, {LF, LR, RM} move together in one direction while {LM, RF, RR} move in the other direction, the second group phase-lagged by 180 degrees hence this group moves backwards while the first group moves forwards. Here's another way of representing the gaits.

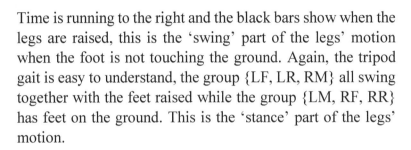

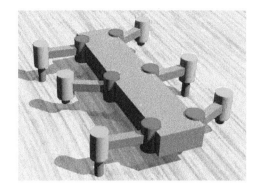

Figure 9.12 Hexapod robot showing legs and feet. It's executing a tripod gait

Time is running to the right and the black bars show when the legs are raised, this is the 'swing' part of the legs' motion when the foot is not touching the ground. Again, the tripod gait is easy to understand, the group {LF, LR, RM} all swing together with the feet raised while the group {LM, RF, RR} has feet on the ground. This is the 'stance' part of the legs' motion.

Our hexapod robot inhabits Webots[5], you can clearly see its legs and feet (they move up and down) in Fig.9.12.

Now we must design our neural circuit to make these three types of gait happen. We shall use a single Hopf oscillator and drive the front-left (FL) foot and leg with the signal u_1. To drive the other legs, we need to shift the phase of this signal to obtain the phases shown in the diagram above. A glance at this diagram reveals two interesting facts. First the phase difference down the left side between LF, LM and between LM, LR is the same for a particular gait. The actual phase difference (60, 90, 180 degrees) depends on the gait. The second fact is that there is a 180 degree phase shift between contra-lateral limbs (LF-RF, LM-RM and LR-RR). This suggests the following architecture which is quite straightforward.

---

[5] It would be good to get this into Unreal-4

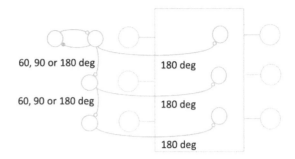

The blue circles represent the robot limbs (legs + feet) and the green circles neurons, or collections of neurons, since we need a chain of 3 neurons to produce a phase shift of 180 degrees. A constant phase shift is produced down the left neurons, then each left neuron is individually phase shifted by 180 degrees and sent to the right. This is much simpler than the coupled oscillator approach used by others.

Let's have a look at some phase plots; we only need to consider the left limbs; the right phases are just mirrored. The diagram below shows a phase difference $\varphi = \pi/3$ (60 degrees) corresponding to the metachronal gait. The black bars show when the foot is lifted, as shown in the gait patterns presented above. So, let's discuss how to get the feet to move; we shall later return to the legs which are tricky buggers.

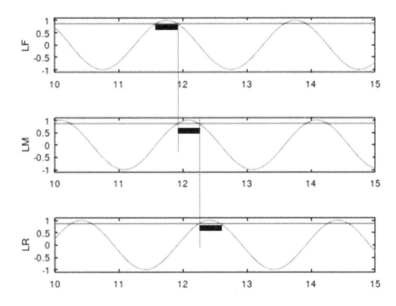

The black bars are correct and represent when signals must be presented to each foot to rise. You can see the red horizontal lines drawn at a particular threshold value, here that is 0.866 for our chosen phase lag value. Our code will tell each foot to rise when the phase is above this threshold. Easy! The only question is, how do we calculate this threshold value? Let's explore this with the help of the following diagram, where the stages in our argument are indicated by yellow blobs.

First (1) We draw the bars when the LF and LM feet are raised. Note that this happens when the phase (blue line) rises above the threshold (red line), which we are trying to discover. Second (2) we identify the phase lag φ between the two feet and also we see the centre of the top sine wave is located at $\pi/2$. Then the important step (3) where we identify the angle where the foot starts to rise. Finally (4) we calculate the value of the threshold for this angle.

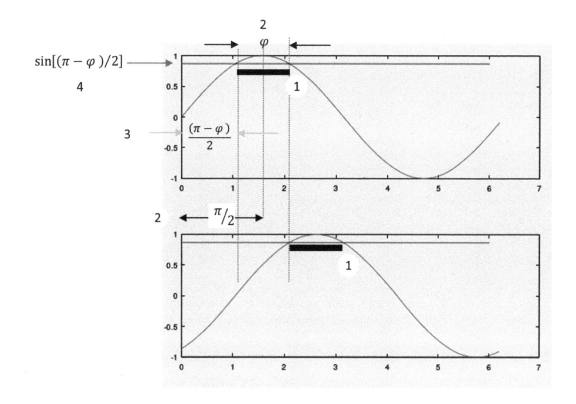

So, we have the expression for the threshold

$$sin[(\pi - \varphi)/2]$$

This is a great result since it is applicable for all three gaits with their own individual phase lags φ, and is easily translated into code, Fig. 9.13.

We now know how to get the feet working. The final piece of the puzzle is to get the legs moving correctly. The legs are driven by the same phases as the feet (before the threshold calculations). Legs have two parts to their motion, a *swing* when the feet are not in contact with the ground, and a *stance* where they are in contact with the ground and so provide propulsion. So, legs and feet have to be coordinated in their motion. Let's have a look at the solution and then see how we got to it.

```
double setFoot(double phase,
double thresh){
if(phase > thresh)
    return UP;
  else
    return DOWN;
}
```

Figure 9.13 Code snipped to raise and lower the feet

The blue curve shows the foot signal; when this rises above the threshold, the foot is up. So, the leg must swing, and this is the red signal which goes from negative (pointing backwards) to positive (pointing forwards). This signal comes from an additional neuron which receives input from the foot neuron *when it is above the threshold*. Here's the code for the additional neuron-17 which drive the LF leg.

```
if( y[0] > thresh)
   drive = 1;
else
   drive = 0;
dydt[17] = (-y[17] + 5.0*drive)/tau1;
```

That completes the development of our hexapod model, it only remains to provide the complete neural circuit.

Chapter 10
Parallel Computing

10.1 A brief Introduction

We are all very familiar with our own PCs, our desktops or laptops, especially the gaming ones with glowing keyboards. Perhaps 'familiar' is not quite the right word; surely, we all have 'personal relationships' with our machines, because we live with them every day. Our own machine is like a spouse, we are effectively married until hardware or software improvement and demands makes us divorce!

What triggers such an event? A significant *economic* cycle where sales of computing devices depend on increase of computing power (operations per second) and increased power enables more complex applications to run. Such applications and the computing power both sit together on a knife edge; the applications use the full power and demand even more. So, computers become more powerful, and the applications become more complex. The knife edge has not disappeared, it has only sharpened.

As developers (and not chip designers) there are a couple of ways we can write our applications to increase their performance. First on a multi-core machine we can write our programs, so they run on all cores simultaneously, this is *multi-processing*. We are thinking of a single box here where the cores *share memory,* and this requires a particular style of parallel programming. We shall not discuss *distributed* parallel processing where each core has its own memory, think about running an application on all PCs in our lab in parallel.

The second approach we can take is to parallelize our application on a *single-core* machine, such as a robot microcontroller, this is *multi-tasking*. This approach to parallel programming provides a strong way of structuring

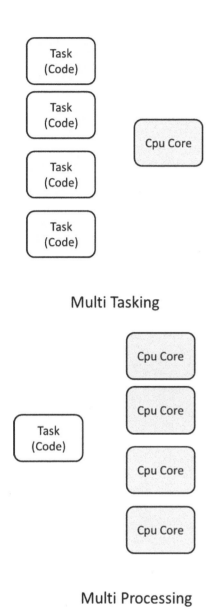

our code most efficiently, cleanly and encourages a more OO structure with resulting code reusability. The two approaches we shall unravel in this chapter are shown in Figure 10.1.

Our study of multitasking will take place using our single core Arduino where we shall look at a couple of features of a *Real Time Operating System* (RTOS) which allows us to run several tasks in parallel and in real time. Application of a RTOS abound in systems driven by microcontrollers, especially those with sensor inputs and actuator outputs. The RTOS allows us to organize our code into coherent units (called *threads*). We can then partition our code into threads, one will handle inputs, another will handle outputs. So this sounds like object-oriented programming in the C-language which is flat not OO. Clearly threads need to communicate with each other, and some may need to respond more quickly than others; the thread reading a sensor value must not miss a reading, so this thread should run at a higher *priority*. All this (and more) is achieved by using a RTOS. Perhaps the closest you have seen to an RTOS is a Finite State Machine, though there are some conceptual differences.

Multiprocessing is a different beast. This is all about how to run *a single program or a single function* on multiple hardware cores. It is not about running a separate program on each core. This involves working with existing code and looking for sections where computations can be done in parallel. Consider the following operation on some arrays.

```
for (int i=0; i<10; i++){
    c[i] = a[i] + b[i];
}
```

It is straightforward to understand how this code can be spread over multiple cores. Say we have 10 cores, then core 1 could compute `c[1] = a[1] + b[1];` and core 2 could compute `c[2] = a[2] + b[2];` and so on. All computations would occur at the same time *in parallel*. So, we have effectively unrolled the loop and spread it over the cores. Nice eh?

Figure 10.1 Distinction between multitasking and multiprocessing.

10.2 Real Time Operating Systems

10.2.1 A Brief Introduction

To understand how a RTOS works on a microcontroller (our Arduino) we need to refresh our understanding of typical microcontroller hardware. Figure 10.2 presents a very simplified description; you can look up the ATmega328 datasheet from Atmel if you like. You recognize the CPU and RAM, also there is I/O electronics, and a timer that can be programmed to emit output pulses. The crucial part for the RTOS is the part of the CPU that handles interrupts. These come from input signals (an input pin may change state from HIGH to LOW) and this change is used to rapidly change which part of the user's program is executed. Here's some Arduino code. In setup() pin 2 is attached to the Interrupts system and is associated with the *interrupt service routine* (ISR) here named **ISR1** That routine is coded at the end. Within loop() there is a call to another function which makes the LEDs blink.

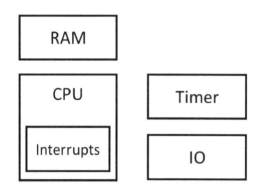

Figure 10.2 Greatly simplified microcontroller system.

```
void setup(){

attachInterrupt(digitalPinToInterrupt(2),ISR1,
CHANGE);
}

void loop(){
  blink_LEDs();
}

void ISR1() {
   bRunning = false;
}
```

So, let's say you have a push button connected to pin 2. If you leave it alone, the code in loop() will merrily churn around. Then you press the button and change the voltage on pin 2. The CPU Interrupts unit recognizes this and *immediately jumps out of the executing loop() code and vectors to the ISR and executes code there.* Then it returns to the loop() code at the point it left off. This happens extremely quickly, on an

ATMega328 it takes 4 CPU clock cycles, running at 16MHz this equates to a quarter of a microsecond! It's also important to note that this code interruption occurs at the level of *machine instructions*. That, as we shall see has some interesting consequences.

Now, an interesting feature of microcontrollers is that their Timers can be used to change the state of an I/O pin. So, if that pin has an interrupt attached, then the timer can raise a periodic interrupt. So, we can write code which will regularly interrupt itself and go off and do something else. This is just what is needed for a RTOS to be able to switch processing from one task to another. Such code forms part of the RTOS *kernel* (core code) and is used to run the RTOS *Scheduler*. Figure 10.3 shows the idea where the red bars show the interrupts generated by the scheduler; when an interrupt occurs, the CPU is vectored to code from either task A or task B in turn. Here I have shown regular *slices* of time.

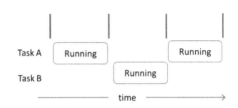

Figure 10.3 Interrupts selecting Task A then Task B to run.

10.2.2 A simple two-task program

Now let's start to add some more detail. Consider the following code comprising 2 tasks. I've omitted task setup code. There are two LEDs attached to the microcontroller; it's easy to see what the code will do. Since Task1 runs for a slice, then Task 2 runs for a slice, then if the time slices are short enough we shall perceive that both tasks run in parallel; LED1 blinks with a period of 1 second and LED2 with a period of 2 seconds.

```
void Task1() {            void Task2() {
   while(1) {                while(1) {
      turnLED1(on);            turnLED2(on);
      delay(500);             delay(1000);
      turnLED1(off);          turnLED2(off);
      delay(500);             delay(1000);
   }                         }
}                          }
```

The timing in Figure 10.3 agrees with this example

10.2.3 The Scheduler

It's clear that a task can exist in one of two states *running* or *not-running*. When a task is running, we say that the scheduler has 'swapped it in' and when it is not running, the scheduler has 'swapped it out'. There is actually a finer distinction; when a task is not running, it exists in one of two substates, *ready* or *blocked.* A *ready* task is ready to be swapped in at the next time slice, on the other hand a *blocked* task is not ready and will not be swapped in. It may be waiting for some input. In this case, the task just swapped out will be immediately swapped in again (providing it is ready!). The task states are shown in Figure 10.4.

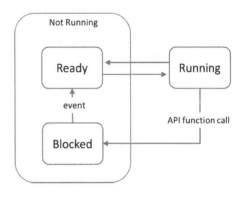

Figure 10.4 States of a Task

Tasks are put into a blocked state using some RTOS API call. for example, a request for a time delay, or waiting for some data to arrive from another task. They can transit to a ready state when some event occurs, like the time delay has expired or data arrives, or there is an external interrupt from a button push.

We can now introduce a more complete timing diagram for the code example presented above.

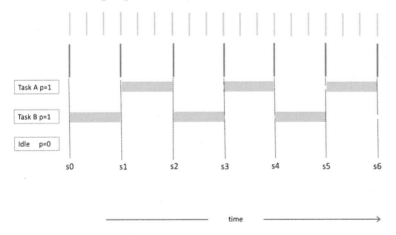

Time is shown running left to right. The green bars show the CPU clock or 'sysTick' and the red bars show the time slices. Horizontal green bars show when the task is running and yellow bars when it is ready. There are no blocked times for either thread. On the left you can see that both tasks have been set to have the same priority. There is also an *Idle Thread* which we'll come onto shortly. Since both threads have the same priority, it is guaranteed that the scheduler will select each thread to run in turn (unless one blocks); this is called the *Round Robin* scheduling algorithm.

Now let's see what happens when the priority of task B is raised.

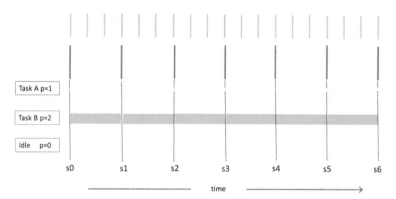

Here both tasks are ready, but the scheduler is guaranteed to swap in the task with higher priority, if both tasks are ready.

While this all sounds reasonable, both situations shown in the timing diagrams above are quite horrible and should never happen. You can see why; at all times the CPU is running a task, it is totally consumed and has no time for anything else. Also, both tasks need to have the same priority to be able to be swapped in. The *cause* of the problem was the calls to the `delay()` function in the code, which simply burned up CPU cycles in some dastardly horrible loop, very bad.

This is where the *blocked* state comes into play. FreeRTOS has an API call `vTaskDelay()` which puts the task into the blocked state for a certain number of ticks, so effectively providing the delay. Here's how you would use it

```
while(1) {
    turnLED1(on);
    vTaskDelay(1000/portTICK_PERIOD_MS);
    turnLED1(off);
    vTaskDelay(1000/portTICK_PERIOD_MS);
}
```

and here's what the timing diagram will look like. Orange represents blocked.

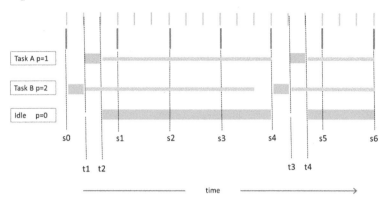

So, what is happening here ? Task B has the higher priority and is ready, so the scheduler swaps this in. It runs and then calls the `vTaskDelay()` API function which puts taskA into the blocked state. The scheduler sees this and also that the lower priority task A is ready, so it swaps it in. Task A then runs until it hits its `vTaskDelay()` function at which point it too blocks and is swapped out.

At this point neither tasks A or B are ready, so the scheduler chooses the Idle Task which you can see runs merrily along. The idle task of lowest priority is created when the scheduler starts up and it is put into the ready state, so it has something to run.

After a while, Task B's delay ends, and it becomes ready so is swapped in at s4. It runs a bit more and at t3 calls its again and re-enters the blocked state. Fortunately, Task A is ready so it can run again.

One more thing; the scheduler is not restricted to do swaps to the time slices s1, s2, … but can also act at sysTick intervals t1, t2, …

10.2.4 More Scheduling Algorithms

This section is moving into advanced territory but is important since we discuss how the majority of microcontroller RTOSs actually are configured. This uses the

Fixed Priority Pre-emptive Scheduling with Time Slicing. In other words, forget Round Robin. What does this mean? Well, 'Fixed Priority' means that the scheduler cannot change the priority of tasks (although tasks may change their priority and that of other tasks). 'Pre-emptive' means that if a low priority task is running and a higher priority task becomes ready, then the lower priority task will be swapped out (even though it does not want to). We know what time slicing is, if two tasks have equal priority then they are swapped at regular time-slice intervals.

You can imagine, the combination of time-slicing and pre-emption is quite powerful. Let's look at a hypothetical set of three tasks to see this in action.

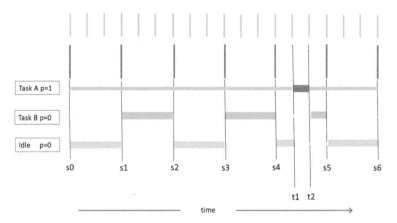

Task B and the Idle task both run at low priority and task A is event-driven and spends most of its time in the blocked state until its event arrives at t1. You can see that the scheduler time-slices task B and the idle task (same priorities) for quite a few slices. But in the middle of slice s4-s5 where idle starts running, task A becomes unblocked, hence ready, and pre-empts the idle task. Task A runs from t1 to t2 to complete its business, then the scheduler chooses to swap the idle task in according to the Round Robin policy.

10.2.5 Possible Issues with Swapping.

There are a couple of potential issues in a multitasking system. The first concerns *shared resources* such as writing to the serial port. Let's say task A wants to print out the string "Hello Cat" and task B wants to print out the string "rapture". Task A starts executing and manages to print "Hello C" then it is swapped out and task B prints "rapture". Then task A is swapped in and completes its output "at". So, what you actually get is "Hello Craptureat". Clearly, we have to protect the printing from a context switch.

Another problem is when 'read, modify, write' operations are encountered. For example, the following C-code reads the value of the variable **max** stored in memory, then ORs the value with 0x01, then writes the value back to the memory. The assembler code is also shown

```
max = max | fred;

LOAD R1, [#max]
LOAD R2, [#fred]
OR R1, R2
STORE R1, [#max]
```

The problem comes from the fact that a single line of C-code produces 4 lines of assembler (therefore machine code) and it is this code that is interrupted by the scheduler. Consider the case where task A and task B attempt to modify the same variable **portA**

- Task A loads the value of **max** into R1
- It is then pre-empted by task B. The scheduler saves all of taskA register values including R1 which contains the value of **max**
- Task B runs all 4 lines of machine code (read, modify, write) and updates **portA** then blocks.
- Task A is swapped in and its registers restored including R1 which contains the old value of **max**
- Task A runs to completion and update the value of **max** then writes it back.

The trouble is task A has used an out-of-date value for **max** and it overwrites the value calculated by task B.

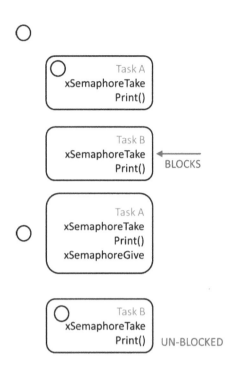

Figure 10.5 Yellow Mutex gives Task A exclusive access to the printer since Task B gets itself blocked.

To prevent these issues, we must protect critical sections of code from being accessed by more than one task. The crudest is to use the critical section construct. In the example below a print statement is wrapped in a couple of macros. These compile into code which disable interrupts and therefore suspends the scheduler.

```
taskENTER_CRITICAL();
    Serial.println("Hello Cat");
taskEXIT_CRITICAL();
```

Turning off interrupts is never a good thing it renders the microcontroller blind to its inputs, and so it may miss a critical event, such as a warning of an impending collision.

A better way is to use a semaphore called a Mutex (from mutual exclusion). Think of a mutex as a single token which only one task can possess at any time, shown in Figure 10.5 as a yellow ball. Initially no task has the mutex, then task A tries to take it and it succeeds. It then calls its print() function. Shortly after, as task A is in the middle of its printing, task B wants to print, so it tries to take the mutex. But it can't (since task A has it) so task B enters the blocked state. When task A has completed printing, it returns the mutex, then it is given to task B which unblocks and does its printing.

10.2.6 A few loose threads

Reading around the subject, you might come across different terminology, some texts refer to 'threads' where we have referred to 'tasks'. Another name for 'swapping in and out' is 'context switching'. We have only hinted at what actually happens during a context switch. Remember this occurs at machine instruction level, so the exact state of the machine needs to be saved (the contents of its registers, any local variables and the instruction pointer) before it's swapped out. Only then can the task be later restored. This saving is done using a stack located in each thread.

10.3. Multiprocessing with OpenMP

10.3.1 A Brief Introduction

While there are many supercomputer architectures, two significant 'poles' of design stand out. First is the 'shared memory' architecture. Here the fundamental design principle is to share memory between each processor. While each processor has its own local cache (system) there is shared memory available to all processors Fig.10.6 (top) and that's where they collaborate. For example, if several processors update individual elements of a vector in parallel, then that vector will be in shared memory. OpenMP supports a shared memory architecture and provides the ability to set up teams of processing threads (operating on different processors) and share the work between them. OpenMP is not a language, as we shall see it comprises a number of compiler 'directives' which the programmer uses to identify regions of code they wish to parallelize.

The other end of the pole is 'distributed memory' such as in a networked or 'cluster' processing configuration, Fig.10.6 (bottom). Here, a different programming model is needed, which is referred to as 'message passing'. Since memory is not shared, each nodes needs to message other nodes to coordinate processing of variables. The industry standard is 'MPI' which is often used by the hi-tech community where clusters of machines (serious boxes the size of a sub-post office) are common.

MPI programming can be tricky and normally requires re-programming of existing code to parallelize it, and certainly does not support an incremental port from sequential to parallel code. It is here that OpenMP shines, since (as mentioned) it consists of a set of 'directives' which the developer can add into existing code, to tell the compiler what sections should be parallelized. Visual Studio has OpenMP built in for C, C++ and Fortran, not for C#. So, you can write parallel programs, today!

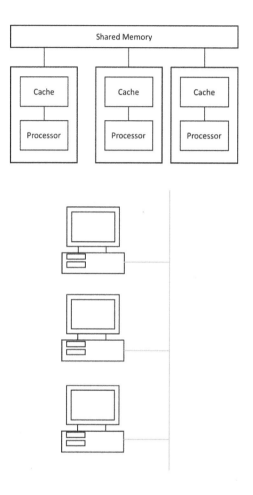

Figure 10.6 Shared memory (top) and distributed memory (bottom) multiprocessing architectures

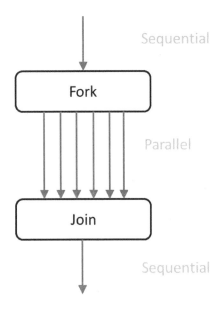

Figure 10.7 Fork-Join software architecture

10.3.2 The OpenMP Model

The OpenMP API consists of a number of 'directives' that tell the compiler when and how to parallelize code; we shall see some of these below. These directives take the form of #pragma statements, inserted into existing sequential code to parallelize it. In addition, OpenMP provides the programmer with (i) the means to create a 'team' of threads, (ii) structures to enable work sharing between the team members, (iii) specification whether variables are *shared* across all threads, or *private* to each thread, and of course (iv) a load of ways to synchronize all of this. OpenMP uses a 'fork-join' approach to execution which you may be familiar with if you were brought up on UNIX. This is shown in Fig.10.7 where the program execution flow starts from top and runs to bottom. Starting with one processing thread, there is a *fork* which creates a team of threads and does some useful work in parallel. When this is done, all threads agree to rendezvous at a point in time and to *join* after which one thread takes over the processing which becomes sequential again. For example, the initial sequential part could be to gather user input, the parallel part could be a multi-body simulation, and the final serial part could be the output of the body final positions.

Let's have a look at a couple of important OpenMP *directives*, and then give some examples along the way.

10.3.3 The Parallel Construct

To move from a single sequential thread and create a *team* of threads *(fork)* running in parallel we wrap the code we wish to parallelize, inside this construct.

```
#pragma omp parallel
{

    our existing code which we want to run in parallel

}
```

At the end of this parallel region there is an implied *barrier* which forces all threads in the team to wait until they have completed their work. Then one thread will take on the remaining sequential programming. While this construct guarantees we have a team of threads, it does not specify how their work is to be shared. There are four work-sharing constructs, we shall encounter only a couple.

10.3.4 The Loop Construct

This is perhaps the most useful and important way to parallelize programs. Just think of how many loops you code on a daily basis. Here's how you would parallelize your loop. Let's say you have this in your existing code

```
for(i=0; i < 4; i++) {
    a[i] = b[i]*c[i];
}
```

In your sequential code a single core would calculate the value of **a[i]** in turn. So, it would calculate **a[0]**, then **a[1]**, then **a[2]**, then **a[3]**. That works fine. But we can do this 4 times as fast if we use 4 cores, where one core calculates each **a[i]**. Here's how we use the **#pragma omp for** construct.

```
#pragma omp parallel
{
    #pragma omp for
    for(i=0; i < 4; i++) {
        a[i] = b[i]*c[i];
    }
}
```

Here we first declare a parallel region **#pragma omp parallel**. Then we indicate that our for loop is to be parallelized using the **#pragma omp for** directive.

So, what does this do? Say we have 4 cores on our machine. The following happens in parallel

core 0 calculates **a[0]**
core 1 calculates **a[1]**
core 2 calculates **a[2]**
core 3 calculates **a[3]**

So, we have obtained a x4 speedup in our computations, and we have done this by 'wrapping' our existing code in a couple of OpenMP compiler directives.

10.3.5 The Sections Construct

This is perhaps a little easier to understand than parallelizing loops (but perhaps not as useful). The idea is that we may have sections of our code which are independent. Yep, think *functions*. Let's say we have two functions in our code which we call sequentially like this

```
main() {
    func1();
    func2();
}
```

If we have two threads (or more) then we can execute both functions in parallel effectively assigning the processing of each function to an independent thread. Here we make use of the *sections* construct, placing this in a parallel region

```
#pragma omp parallel
{

    #pragma omp sections
    {
        #pragma omp section
        func1();
        #pragma omp section
        func2();
    }
}
```

So, one thread will execute **funct1()** *at the same time* as the second thread is executing **funct2().** One potential problem called 'load imbalance' occurs which reduces the parallelization speed-up. If one function has more work to do than the other, then the second thread will be hanging around waiting for the first, effectively doing nothing. Also, if you had 5 functions and only 4 threads then one thread would do twice the amount of work and the other 3 would be twiddling their thumbs.

10.3.6 The Barrier Construct

A barrier is a point in the execution of code where all threads wait for each other; no thread is allowed to proceed until all threads have reached the barrier. While there is an *explicit* barrier construct **#pragma omp barrier** which can be inserted into code, other constructs provide an *implied* barrier which provides us with some very useful synchronization tools. Consider the code below which effectively contains two sections! In the first, the values of vector **a[i]** are initialized in parallel, *then when all have been initialized,* they are used in the second section in some computation.

```
#pragma omp parallel
{
    #pragma omp for
    for(i=0;i<N;i++)
        a[i] = i;

    #pragma omp for
    for(i=0;i<N;i++)
        b[i] = 2*a[i];

}
```

Here there is an *implied* barrier at the end of the first **omp for** so all the values of **a[i]** are initialized before they are used in the second **omp for**.

One case where a barrier can be explicitly used is in our classic read-modify-write situation, which we could protect using a critical section or semaphore. If we inserted a barrier between writes to and read from a shared variable, that would avoid a data-race condition.

10.3.7 When OpenMP goes wrong or can't ever work.

Code which cannot be parallelized.

Let's compare the two loops shown below. The first can be parallelized but the second cannot.

```
for(i=0;i<N;i++)
    a[i] = a[i] + b[i];
```

```
for(i=0;i<N;i++)
    a[i] = a[i+1] + b[i];
```

In the first loop, the iterations are independent, and so can be shared across a whole team of threads, each thread dealing with the i'th update. The second loop has a dependency; the value of **a[i]** depends on the next value in the array **a[i]**. Say one thread is updating **a[i]** and expects to find the value of **a[i+1]** *at that time.* It might find it, but it might not, because another thread may have already updated **a[i+1];** We just can't know. If we ran this code, it might work correctly but it might not; the behaviour is non-deterministic. This is another example of a *data race* condition, here introduced by an incorrect parallelization of a loop.

Thread-Safe and non-Thread-Safe Functions

We have stressed that one strength of OpenMP is that it allows us to use existing code. More than likely, our code uses a library containing functions which we have not written, and so have no idea what is in the library. In particular we may not know if the library makes use of global variables. This can lead to a problem. Here's a toy example. The main function calls a single library function which updates a global variable.

```
int nastyGlobal;

void lib_func() {
    nastyGlobal++;
```

```
        // some meaningful stuff
}

main() {
      #pragma omp parallel
      {
            lib_func();
      }
}
```

Since we are calling the library function from a parallel region multiple threads may try to access **nastyGlobal** at the same time; we have a read-modify-write operation. Here the problem is easily solved putting the update into a critical region,

```
void lib_func() {
      #pragma omp critical
      nastyGlobal++;
      // some meaningful stuff
}
```

CPSIA information can be obtained
at www.ICGtesting.com
Printed in the USA
LVHW072333110722
723217LV00017B/578